Dorchester, and later, Weymouth, specialising in the restoration of local churches. Hardy used his knowledge as an architect in *Far from the Madding Crowd*: in the precise, detailed descriptions of Bathsheba's house Upper Weatherbury Farm and Weatherbury church.

Marriage

In 1870 – the year his first novel *Desperate Remedies* was completed – he met and fell in love with Emma Lavinia Gifford, when he was supervising the restoration of St Juliot's church in North Cornwall. He admired her energy and vitality, possibly using some of these qualities to portray Bathsheba.

When, in 1872, Hardy was offered £400 for serialisation of *Far from the Madding Crowd*, he gave up his job to write full time and lived at home in Bockhampton 'within a walk of the district in which the incidents are supposed to occur'. He stressed the 'great advantage to be actually among the people described at the time of describing them'. A year later when Hardy was still writing the novel, Horace Moule committed suicide, an event which possibly inspires Boldwood's tragic murder of Troy and attempted suicide at the end of the novel.

In the novel Bathsheba's marriage to Troy also becomes unhappy.

In 1874 Hardy married Emma. They lived in various parts of Dorset and London, finally settling at Max Gate, a grand house Hardy designed for himself near Dorchester. He wrote many other novels including *The Mayor of Casterbridge* (1886). Despite fame and literary success, Hardy's marriage became increasingly unhappy. When his later novels *Tess of the d'Urbervilles* and *Jude the Obscure* were criticised as obscene and immoral, Hardy gave up novel-writing and wrote poetry instead. After Emma's death in 1912, racked with remorse, he revisited the scenes of their courtship in Cornwall and wrote much of his best poetry, notably 'Beeny Cliff'.

Second
marriage

In 1914 he married Florence Dugdale, his secretary. Together they destroyed Emma's diaries and other private papers, and produced an official biography of Hardy before his death. After the First World War Hardy became more pessimistic and depressed. He died in 1928, aged 87. His heart was buried in Stinsford Church and his ashes in Poets' Corner, Westminster Abbey.

CONTEXT & SETTING

Rural life

Hardy gives a
realistic view of
rural poverty.

Hardy wrote the novel in 1872 but set it in the 1840s and he stated his intention in his Preface of recording 'a vanishing way of life'. Hardy introduces us to a wide section of Weatherbury society, from Boldwood, a gentleman farmer, to farm labourers and a poor pregnant homeless character, Fanny, who dies in Casterbridge workhouse. He describes rural customs such as the hiring of servants on Old Candlemas Day.

Weatherbury's model, Puddletown, had two inns and two beer houses. In the novel Hardy describes Warren's Malthouse where the men drink and exchange gossip. In fact drunkenness in rural places was a problem in Victorian times. The 1840s were a time of acute rural poverty. Labourers were paid very little, had large families and lived in crowded cottages, cooking over a grimy open hearth. They had no piped water, flush toilets or lights except for smoky candles and oil lamps. The landlord dominated their lives and could evict them by refusing to renew their lease. Organised attempts to improve conditions were repressed. In 1834 six labourers from Tolpuddle had been transported to Australia for trying to set up an agricultural union. The Dorset labourers wanted to get their low wages of seven shillings a week raised to ten,

CONTENTS

PREFACE

York Notes are designed to give you a broader perspective on works of literature studied at GCSE and equivalent levels. We have carried out extensive research into the needs of the modern literature student prior to publishing this new edition. Our research showed that no existing series fully met students' requirements. Rather than present a single authoritative approach, we have provided alternative viewpoints, empowering students to reach their own interpretations of the text. York Notes provide a close examination of the work and include biographical and historical background, summaries, glossaries, analyses of characters, themes, structure and language, cultural connections and literary terms.

If you look at the Contents page you will see the structure for the series. However, there's no need to read from the beginning to the end as you would with a novel, play, poem or short story. Use the Notes in the way that suits you. Our aim is to help you with your understanding of the work, not to dictate how you should learn.

York Notes are written by English teachers and examiners, with an expert knowledge of the subject. They show you how to succeed in coursework and examination assignments, guiding you through the text and offering practical advice. Questions and comments will extend, test and reinforce your knowledge. Attractive colour design and illustrations improve clarity and understanding, making these Notes easy to use and handy for quick reference.

York Notes are ideal for:
- Essay writing
- Exam preparation
- Class discussion

The author of these Notes is Nicky Alper BA, PGCE, a GCSE coursework moderator and examiner, who has also published Notes on Alan Ayckbourn's *Absent Friends*. She teaches English at a leading girls' independent school in Dorset and has walked over much of the landscape Hardy describes.

The text used in these Notes is the Penguin Classics Edition, edited and with an introduction and notes by Ronald Blythe (1978, 1985).

> *Health Warning:* This study guide will enhance your understanding, but should not replace the reading of the original text and/or study in class.

PART ONE

INTRODUCTION

HOW TO STUDY A NOVEL

You have bought this book because you wanted to study a novel on your own. This may supplement classwork.

- You will need to read the novel several times. Start by reading it quickly for pleasure, then read it slowly and carefully. Further readings will generate new ideas and help you to memorise the details of the story.
- Make careful notes on themes, plot and characters of the novel. The plot will change some of the characters. Who changes?
- The novel may not present events chronologically. Does the novel you are reading begin at the beginning of the story or does it contain flashbacks and a muddled time sequence? Can you think why?
- How is the story told? Is it narrated by one of the characters or by an all-seeing ('omniscient') narrator?
- Does the same person tell the story all the way through? Or do we see the events through the minds and feelings of a number of different people?
- Which characters does the narrator like? Which characters do you like or dislike? Do your sympathies change during the course of the book? Why? When?
- Any piece of writing (including your notes and essays) is the result of thousands of choices. No book had to be written in just one way: the author could have chosen other words, other phrases, other characters, other events. How could the author of your novel have written the story differently? If events were recounted by a minor character how would this change the novel?

Studying on your own requires self-discipline and a carefully thought-out work plan in order to be effective. Good luck.

Early life

Thomas Hardy was born in Dorset in 1840 – at Higher Bockhampton in the village of Stinsford, two miles from Dorchester, the county town which Hardy renamed Casterbridge in his novels. He lived in a cob cottage; both his grandfather and father were stone masons, who played 'cello and violin in the church band. Hardy, too, learned to play the violin. In *Far from the Madding Crowd* Gabriel Oak sings bass in the church choir and plays the flute. As a boy Hardy visited many of his relatives in the nearby village of Puddletown, which becomes Weatherbury in *Far from the Madding Crowd*.

Studies at Dorchester

Notice how Hardy uses his knowledge of architecture in the novel.

At the age of ten he was sent to school in Dorchester where he learned Latin. When he was sixteen, he started work for Hicks, a Dorchester architect. He continued to live at home, studying classics early each morning before he walked to work. William Barnes, the Dorset poet, had a school next door to Hicks's office and Hardy became a friend of his. In *Far from the Madding Crowd* Hardy quotes some of Barnes's **dialect** poetry (see Literary Terms) and he adopted Barnes's name of Wessex for the area he wrote about. He also met and befriended Horace Moule, who helped him study Greek and guided his other reading.

There are many echoes of local happenings in *Far from the Madding Crowd*. Hardy watched a woman hanged at Dorchester prison for the murder of her husband: in the novel a scaffold is erected at Casterbridge gaol in preparation for hanging Boldwood. Dorchester workhouse became the Casterbridge Union where Fanny dies. The cornmarket where Bathsheba trades as a farmer is another Dorchester building.

Hardy as architect

When Hardy qualified in 1862 he went to work in London, where he started to write poetry. His health suffered, so he returned to work for Hicks in the average in the rest of the country. Many agricultural labourers emigrated to escape the depression of the 1850s. Gabriel in the novel considers emigrating to California.

Farming

In the 1840s farming was labour-intensive; mechanisation started later in the 1860s. Half of Puddletown's labourers were employed in agriculture; like them, Hardy's characters' lives are bound by the seasons. We see Gabriel caring for his pregnant ewes

When you read the novel, notice how the characters' lives are influenced by the weather and the seasons.

and the weak lambs. Barley and corn are planted in the spring and harvested in late summer. Most working people wore traditional dress: Gabriel, the farmer, wears a 'low-crowned felt hat' (p. 52), an overcoat, leather leggings, large boots and a big watch. Later, when he courts Bathsheba, he adds a flowered waistcoat and a handkerchief and oils his hair. After losing his sheep, and having to seek work as a shepherd, the penniless Gabriel dons smock dress and crook, while Bathsheba, becoming the mistress of a farm, exchanges the cheap bright cotton clothes of the cottager for rich silks.

Social values

Lesley Stephen, editor of the *Cornhill Magazine* which was serialising the novel, was aware that his conservative readers were easily shocked. He suggested that Hardy treat Troy's seduction of Fanny 'gingerly'. In the original serialised version of the novel, Bathsheba looks at Fanny's illegitimate baby in the coffin, at its 'face so delicately small' and the 'plump backs of its little fists'. In the later version, this passage was censored: Bathsheba only learns about the baby when Liddy 'whispered ... into her ear' (p. 353).

Religion was an important and integral part of people's lives in Victorian times. Gabriel proves Troy is a hypocrite when he pretends to go to church by a secret door.

Topography   Most of the events in the novel take place in the five-mile stretch of the old road between Dorchester and Puddletown.

- The farmhouses. Druce Farm is the model for Boldwood's Little Weatherbury Farm. Hardy used the fine old Jacobean house, Waterson Manor, for Bathsheba's Upper Weatherbury Farm, moving the houses one mile nearer. He describes the architectural features with precise detail.
- Puddletown church is renamed Weatherbury church. In it is a minstrels' gallery, where Hardy's father and grandfather actually played with the Puddletown musicians. In the novel Gabriel sings in the choir in the gallery. There are box pews, on one of which is carved the name Henery, with the extra 'e' like Henery Fray, Bathsheba's labourer. The churchyard has a secluded corner shaded by yews like the place

Consider why   where Fanny is buried. In the south-east corner is a
Hardy thinly   gargoyle that once leaked, like the one that washed
disguises real places.   away the flowers on Fanny's grave. The hideous appearance of this gargoyle is thought to be based on one in Stinsford church, near Hardy's cottage in Bockhampton. In *Far from the Madding Crowd* Troy sleeps in the stone porch protected from the rain.

- Troytown (Roy-town), the nearby hamlet, suggested the name Troy to Hardy. At the Bucks Head inn Joseph Poorgrass broke his journey with Fanny's coffin and got drunk.
- Yellowham Wood became Yalbury Wood in the novel. Here the scared Joseph Poorgrass called out 'Man-a-lost' (p. 108); when an owl hooted in reply, he is said to have answered, 'Joseph Poorgrass of Weatherbury, sir!'
- At Yellowham Hill (Yalbury Hill) Troy and Bathsheba, driving at dusk, meet Fanny struggling on foot.

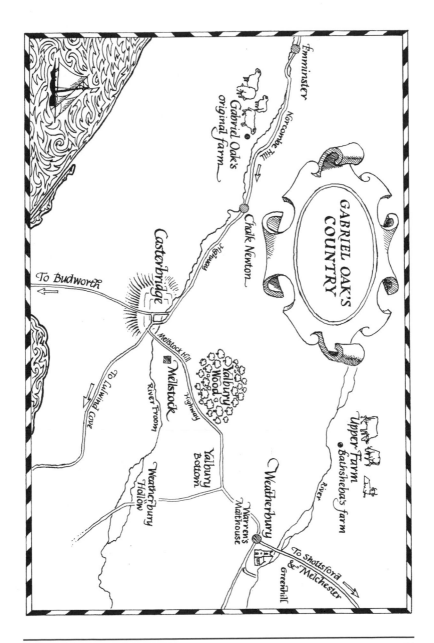

PART TWO

SUMMARIES

GENERAL SUMMARY

Chapters 1–5
Gabriel's
proposal

Farmer Gabriel first meets Bathsheba at Norcombe Hill; he pays her fare at the turnpike. He meets her again when he is lambing and she is looking after her aunt's cows. She saves Gabriel from suffocation in his lambing hut. He falls in love and proposes, but she firmly rejects him. Soon afterwards she goes away to Weatherbury. Gabriel loses his flock of uninsured sheep over a precipice and is ruined.

Chapters 6–19
Boldwood's
proposal

Two months later Gabriel, on his way to find work, puts out a fire at a Weatherbury farm. He discovers that he has saved Bathsheba's crops; she is now managing her dead uncle's farm. She employs him as her shepherd. Gabriel gives money to a girl (Fanny) who insists on secrecy. Bathsheba's bailiff is caught stealing and sacked. Bathsheba sends men to search for the missing Fanny. She decides to manage the farm herself without a bailiff. Fanny arrives at her soldier-lover Troy's barracks pleading with him to marry her.

At Casterbridge cornmarket all the farmers except Boldwood admire Bathsheba. Bathsheba sends Boldwood a Valentine as a joke. He dreams about Bathsheba. The next morning at Warren's Malthouse Boldwood gives Gabriel a letter from Fanny which he has opened by mistake. Fanny writes of her forthcoming marriage to Troy. On her wedding day she muddles the churches, and Troy, having waited over an hour, refuses to marry her. Boldwood falls in love with Bathsheba and proposes; she tries to refuse him.

Chapters 20–33 *Troy's courtship, Boldwood's rejection*	Gabriel criticises Bathsheba for sending the Valentine, so she sacks him. The next day her sheep break into the clover and become sick. She is forced to recall Gabriel to save the flock and he agrees to stay on as shepherd. Boldwood meets Bathsheba at the great barn; Gabriel accidentally wounds the sheep he is shearing.

At the shearing supper Bathsheba sings, accompanied by Gabriel's flute. Later Boldwood proposes again. That night, inspecting the farm outside, Bathsheba's dress becomes entangled on a strange soldier's (Troy's) spur. Next day Troy helps with the haymaking and continues to flatter Bathsheba. He helps her hive the bees. That evening she goes to a secret rendezvous and is thrilled by Troy's sword exercise. Gabriel warns Bathsheba not to trust Troy; she tries to sack him again.

Troy goes to Bath and Bathsheba sends Boldwood a letter rejecting him. On her way to visit Liddy, she meets Boldwood. He reproaches Bathsheba, and threatens to kill Troy. Bathsheba leaves secretly for Bath, intending to warn Troy and renounce him.

Chapters 34–46 *Marriage and separation*	Boldwood bribes Troy to marry Fanny first and then Bathsheba, only to discover that Troy has already married Bathsheba. He vows revenge.

At the harvest supper Troy ignores Gabriel's warnings to cover the ricks against the approaching storm. The men become drunk and unconscious with the strong drink Troy forces on them. Gabriel covers the ricks assisted by Bathsheba carrying reeds up a ladder. However, all Boldwood's ricks are uncovered and damaged.

Bathsheba and Troy quarrel; he has lost money gambling on horses. They meet Fanny walking to Casterbridge. Troy arranges a secret meeting with Fanny. She struggles onwards collapsing on the workhouse steps. She dies giving birth to an illegitimate baby which also dies. Bathsheba is angered by Troy's refusal to destroy Fanny's lock of hair. Troy waits in vain for Fanny at Grey's Bridge. Bathsheba sends Joseph Poorgrass to collect Fanny's coffin, but he gets drunk and the funeral has to be postponed.

Bathsheba opens the coffin, left in her house overnight, to discover Fanny with the baby. She now knows Fanny was Troy's former lover. When Troy returns they quarrel. Bathsheba runs away, remaining outdoors until after Fanny's funeral. At Casterbridge Troy buys a tombstone, and plants flowers on Fanny's grave, which are washed away that night by heavy rain. Next morning Bathsheba discovers Troy has left her.

Chapters 47–57 Endings

Troy is presumed drowned in Lulwind Cove. His clothes are found, but he was actually rescued by a passing boat. Bathsheba instinctively feels Troy is still alive. Gabriel becomes Bathsheba's bailiff and manages Boldwood's farm with a small share in the profits. At Greenhill Fair Troy reappears. He spies on Bathsheba and intercepts a note informing Bathsheba of his presence. Boldwood proposes again. Bathsheba postpones a reply, confiding her fears for Boldwood's sanity in Gabriel.

At Christmas Boldwood holds a party. Anticipating Bathsheba's acceptance, he has already bought an engagement ring. Bathsheba under pressure agrees to marry him in six years' time if Troy fails to reappear. When Troy arrives at Boldwood's party and attempts to reclaim Bathsheba, Boldwood shoots Troy dead and attempts suicide. He surrenders himself and is imprisoned in Casterbridge gaol. Bathsheba prepares Troy's body for burial, then collapses. Boldwood's death sentence is commuted to life imprisonment after an appeal.

Bathsheba sinks into depression and is shocked at Gabriel's decision to emigrate. She calls on Gabriel to dissuade him and prompts his second successful proposal. They are married quietly soon afterwards.

DETAILED SUMMARIES

CHAPTERS 1–5: GABRIEL'S PROPOSAL

CHAPTER 1

Note how Hardy presents his hero.

Farmer Gabriel is twenty-eight and unmarried. He leases a sheep farm at Norcombe Hill. Looking over a hedge his eye is caught by an attractive dark-haired girl sitting in a wagon, admiring her reflection in a looking-glass. At the turnpike the girl argues about the price; Gabriel pays. She drives away without thanking him.

COMMENT

Gabriel is a man of 'sound judgement' (p. 51) and 'quiet modesty' (p. 52). He wears large practical garments, while Bathsheba's clothes are gay and bright. His immediate attraction to Bathsheba is contrasted to her indifference.

GLOSSARY

Laodicean a person with moderate religious feelings

turnpike gate a place where travellers pay a fee or toll

CHAPTER 2

Think about how Gabriel observes Bathsheba.

A few days later Gabriel is playing his flute, spending the night in his lambing hut, watching over his ewes. He carries a weak, new-born lamb back to the hut to revive it by the fire and then returns it to its mother. He notices a light in a nearby shed, and observes two women tending two cows and a calf. He recognises Bathsheba whose hat has blown away. She rides off at dawn to fetch oatmeal for the cows.

COMMENT

Gabriel, by his own industry, has risen from shepherd to bailiff to independent sheep farmer, although the farm is only leased and he has borrowed money to buy the sheep.

Gabriel admires Bathsheba's beauty. It is fate that he sees her again at Norcombe Hill; they are both tending new-born animals.

Bathsheba wishes to be rich enough to 'pay a man' (p. 63) to tend the cows. This is **prophetic irony** (see Literary Terms). She is unconventional, careless of her lost hat and prepared to ride without a side-saddle.

GLOSSARY   **St Thomas's day** the shortest day of the year in December
Lucina Roman goddess of childbirth

CHAPTER 3   At daylight Bathsheba returns. Gabriel, having retrieved her hat, stares at her from his hut, fascinated by her gymnastics on the horse. When he restores the hat, she is embarrassed, realising she's been observed. The following five days she returns to tend the cows.

Note Bathsheba's attitude to Gabriel.

Inside his lambing hut Gabriel has gone to sleep by the fire without opening the ventilating slide; Bathsheba luckily hears his dog howling outside and saves Gabriel from suffocation by throwing warm milk over him. She refuses to give her name, but allows Gabriel to hold her hand, even suggesting he can kiss it.

COMMENT   Bathsheba is unconventional, enjoying the free movement on the horse's back. Her manner is flirtatious.

Gabriel is grateful for his rescue. He's also practical, telling her the exact value of the hut.

GLOSSARY   **Nymphean** like a goddess
yeaning lambing

CHAPTER 4   Gabriel, dismayed to learn Bathsheba's visits will end when the cow runs dry, decides to marry her. He dresses neatly and oils his hair, calling on her aunt with

Consider how Hardy presents Gabriel's proposal. the gift of a lamb. He bluntly states his intentions. The aunt deters Gabriel by emphasising Bathsheba's superior education and many sweethearts. Gabriel leaves. Bathsheba runs after him, assuring him there are no rivals. Gabriel asks her directly, offering his 'nice snug little farm' (p. 77) and tempting her with the prospect of a piano, a gig and babies. The penniless Bathsheba is momentarily tempted, but she doesn't love him and prefers her freedom. He promises to be faithful, despite the rejection. She rebuffs him and he decides to 'ask you no more' (p. 82).

COMMENT Gabriel's proposal is a mixture of romance and practicality. He honestly presents his financial situation, offering to 'work twice as hard' (p. 78). He sees Bathsheba as superior because she talks like a 'lady' (p. 81) and her uncle is a tenant farmer.

Bathsheba is romantic. Gabriel is an eligible suitor for a poor girl, but she prefers her independence.

She was 'too wild' (p. 76) to be a governess, the conventional occupation for a well-educated penniless girl.

GLOSSARY

guano and Roman cement the yellow-white excrement of seabirds and the darker yellow of Roman building material

Commination-service a church service read on Ash Wednesday, containing threats

CHAPTER 5 Bathsheba moves to Weatherbury. One morning Gabriel is awakened by sheep bells. He runs out to discover all 200 of his pregnant ewes dead at the bottom of a chalk pit. They were chased by an *Note how Hardy builds up tension.* inexperienced sheep dog. Gabriel mourns their loss and then realises the ewes were uninsured. He shoots the errant sheep dog. After selling his stock and equipment to pay his debts, he is penniless.

GABRIEL'S PROPOSAL

COMMENT   It is fate that despite Gabriel's efforts to better himself
he loses all his sheep and is ruined.

He is 'intensely humane' (p. 86), pitying the dead sheep
and feeling relief that Bathsheba had refused him and
thus won't have to share his 'poverty' (p. 86).

Note the use of **pathetic fallacy** (see Literary Terms &
Style) in the description at the end of the chapter.

GLOSSARY   **staple** unmanufactured wool
Hylas son of the king of Mysia who fell in a river and was
drowned

A Identify the speaker.

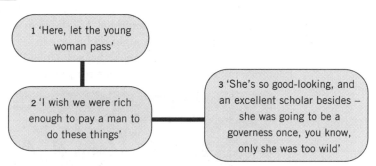

1 'Here, let the young woman pass'

2 'I wish we were rich enough to pay a man to do these things'

3 'She's so good-looking, and an excellent scholar besides – she was going to be a governess once, you know, only she was too wild'

Identify the person 'to whom' this comment refers.

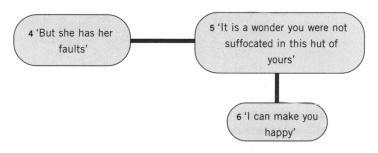

4 'But she has her faults'

5 'It is a wonder you were not suffocated in this hut of yours'

6 'I can make you happy'

Check your answers on page 89.

B Consider these issues.

a Notice how Hardy evokes the reader's sympathy and admiration for his workaday hero Gabriel Oak in the opening chapters.

b Consider how Hardy creates an atmosphere of mystery around Bathsheba. We see events largely through Gabriel's eyes.

c Look again at Gabriel's proposal. Find evidence for the combination of romance and practicality.

d Think about how the mood of the novel darkens in Chapter 5.

CHAPTERS 6–19: BOLDWOOD'S PROPOSAL

CHAPTER 6   Two months later Gabriel fails to find work as either a
bailiff or a shepherd at Casterbridge. He sleeps in a
wagon at Weatherbury that night on his way to
Shottsford hiring fair. Waking, he hears Joseph
Poorgrass talking about his new mistress, Bathsheba.

Note how Hardy   Gabriel walks on and sees a straw rick on fire. He calms
creates mystery   the panicking farmhands, scales the rick, and beats out
about the owner of   the flames with his crook, preventing the fire spreading.
the farm.   He then discovers that Bathsheba is the new mistress of
the farm: her uncle has recently died. She arrives on
horseback and he asks her for work as a shepherd.

COMMENT   Roles are reversed: Gabriel repays Bathsheba for saving
his life by saving her crops; Bathsheba is now his
superior – mistress of her own farm, while Gabriel
seeks employment.

Gabriel is brave and calm in a crisis in contrast to Troy
later (Chapter 38).

GLOSSARY   **hiring fair** on Candlemas Day domestic and farm servants were
hired for the coming year
Siddim pits in the Dead Sea into which the defeated Kings of
Sodom and Gomorrah fell

CHAPTER 7

Consider how Hardy shrouds Fanny's character in mystery.

Bathsheba employs Gabriel as her shepherd. Gabriel is amazed at the way she's changed from 'unpractised girl' to 'supervising and cool woman' (p. 99). He makes his way to Warren's Malthouse to ask about lodgings. In the churchyard he meets a poorly dressed girl (Fanny). When he hands her all his money, he is shocked by her pulse rate. He agrees to keep the meeting secret.

COMMENT

Fanny is a contrast to the well-dressed confident Bathsheba.

There is **prophetic irony** (see Literary Terms) in that Fanny's first and last appearances in the novel are both in Weatherbury churchyard.

Gabriel is skilled at diagnosing sickness in sheep and recognises Fanny's fast pulse rate as a symptom of disease.

GLOSSARY   **Ashtoreth** a heathen goddess

CHAPTER 8

Note the detailed descriptions of Warren's Malthouse and the villagers.

Gabriel is easily accepted by the villagers and invited to use the communal drinking cup. The maltster knew both his father and grandfather. He learns more about Bathsheba's parents and plays his flute. He leaves with Jan Coggan, who has offered him lodgings. At Warren's Malthouse news is brought: Pennyways, Bathsheba's bailiff, has been sacked for stealing, Fanny has been discovered missing. Bathsheba orders the men to make discreet enquiries in Casterbridge about Fanny's soldier lover.

COMMENT

The villagers comment on people and events. They show the prevalence of drunkenness as well as the strong bonds of family and rural tradition.

Gabriel is quickly accepted whereas the workmen later criticise Troy.

Bathsheba feels responsible for Fanny, her youngest servant.

Fanny's destination and the identity of her soldier lover are mysterious.

GLOSSARY   **Elymas-the-Sorcerer** a false prophet punished with temporary blindness, forced to grope for assistance

gay jerry-go-nimble show describing a bright display of booths and acrobats

metheglin (Welsh) spiced mead

Minerva Roman goddess of war, wisdom and the arts

CHAPTER 9

Note the precise architectural description of Bathsheba's house.

Bathsheba assisted by Liddy is so dusty and dishevelled from sorting her uncle's goods that she refuses to see her neighbour, Boldwood, when he calls for news of Fanny. On questioning Liddy she learns that he is handsome, rich and single. He befriended Fanny as a child, paying for her education and finding her a job as servant to Bathsheba's uncle. Bathsheba is cross when she discovers that Coggan's little boy did not contradict Boldwood's assumption that she was old, sober and 'staid' (p. 125). Without naming Gabriel she discloses that she's already had a proposal of marriage. She retires to dress herself, as the workmen arrive.

COMMENT   Boldwood is a highly eligible bachelor, a 'gentleman-farmer' (p. 124). **Ironically** (see Literary Terms) he is described by Liddy as 'a hopeless man for a woman' (p. 124).

Bathsheba while hinting that Gabriel was not 'quite good enough', admits she 'rather liked him' (p. 126).

GLOSSARY   **thirtover** contrary

pucker confusion

Chain Salpae basic forms of marine life

CHAPTER 10

Bathsheba pays her workmen, adding a generous bonus. She intends to manage the farm and supervise the

Consider how Bathsheba establishes her authority.

workers herself without a bailiff. Cain Ball is appointed as Gabriel's assistant. There is news that Fanny followed her lover's regiment when it left Casterbridge.

COMMENT   Gabriel is impressed by Bathsheba's poise, which he attributes to 'the social rise which had advanced her from a cottage to a large house and fields' (p. 131).

The identity of Fanny's lover remains a mystery.

The tune his regiment play leaving Casterbridge 'The girl I left behind me' is **dramatically ironic** (see Literary Terms).

GLOSSARY   **wimbling haybonds** making hay into rope bonds with a wimble (an instrument for boring holes)

gawkhammer stupid

thesmothete (Greek) lawgiver

CHAPTER 11

Hardy evokes pity for Fanny.

On a dark snowy night Fanny arrives at her lover, Troy's barracks. She pleads with him to arrange their marriage. Troy has failed to ask permission from his officers. He agrees to meet her at her lodgings next day.

COMMENT   Hardy uses a framing **device** to **symbolise** (see Literary Terms) Fanny's weak position as suppliant to Troy in the window above.

Hardy dissociates Fanny from the 'bad women' (p. 138), or prostitutes, who follow the regiment.

Troy's first appearance is unfavourable: he seems careless and thoughtless.

The weather and landscape create a doomed atmosphere.

CHAPTER 12

Note Hardy's Bathsheba is the only woman in the cornmarket.
description of the Although 'daintily dressed' (p. 139), she is determined
cornmarket. to brave the stares and drive hard bargains. She is
piqued that Boldwood is the only man indifferent to
her charms. Her curiosity is roused by the rumour that
he has been 'jilted' (p. 143).

COMMENT Bathsheba regards the handsome Boldwood as a
challenge.

There is **prophetic irony** (see Literary Terms) in the
discussion on jilting. Later in Chapter 23 Boldwood
accuses Bathsheba of encouraging and then rejecting
him.

CHAPTER 13

Letters and notes Liddy persuades Bathsheba to play a fortune-telling
are an important game using the Bible to predict who Bathsheba will
device (see Literary marry. Bathsheba also agrees to send a Valentine,
Terms) in the inscribed with the seal 'Marry Me', and bought for a
novel. child, to Boldwood as a joke instead. She wants to
make the 'most dignified and valuable man in the
parish' (p. 147) notice her.

COMMENT The incidents are faintly blasphemous. It is Sunday and
Bathsheba tosses a hymn book to decide whether to
send the Valentine.

Hardy comments on Bathsheba's idle trivial motives,
hinting at the **tragic** (see Literary Terms) effect this has
on the mind and fate of Boldwood, the recipient.

GLOSSARY **Sortes sanctorum** a device using a key in the Bible to cast holy
lots
Daniel the only man who refused to worship the king's golden
statue

CHAPTER 14

Note the effect of the Valentine on Boldwood.

Boldwood stares so intensely at the Valentine that 'the large red seal became as a blot of blood on the retina of his eye' (p. 149). It haunts his dreams. Waking early he watches Gabriel appear over the hill near Bathsheba's farm. Preoccupied, he opens a letter addressed to Gabriel by mistake.

COMMENT

Boldwood's reserved exterior conceals his deep emotional nature.

Hardy adds tension by using **pathetic fallacy** (see Literary Terms & Style).

GLOSSARY

yeoman freeholding farmer
ewe-lease sheep pasture

CHAPTER 15

Hardy again uses a letter as a plot device.

Gabriel carries four new-born lambs to Warren's Malthouse and revives them by the fire. Hearing hostile comments about Bathsheba, he springs to her defence. The workmen placate Gabriel, praising his skills and lamenting that he has not been made bailiff. Boldwood enters and gives Gabriel his letter, which is from Fanny. She repays Gabriel's loan and writes rejoicing in her forthcoming marriage to Troy. Boldwood grieves at Fanny's naïveté. He discloses Troy's family history, describing Troy as 'clever' but 'wild' (p. 161). He follows Gabriel when he leaves, asking him to identify the handwriting on the Valentine. Gabriel recognises Bathsheba's handwriting.

COMMENT

Hardy describes Boldwood's entrance as 'a shade darkened the door' (p. 160), an appropriate **metaphor** (see Literary Terms). He changes the homely relaxed atmosphere.

Fanny's comment 'All has ended well' (p. 160) is premature and **ironic** (see Literary Terms).

Gabriel is a skilled and caring shepherd. He is upset by the discovery that Bathsheba has sent the Valentine.

GLOSSARY   **pipkin** earthenware pot

tined closed

Lady Day the Feast of Annunciation of Our Lady, a quarter day on which agreements were made and rent paid

CHAPTER 16

Consider why Hardy added this chapter after the novel was completed.

Troy waits for Fanny at the church of All Souls for over an hour on their wedding day. As he leaves the church, Fanny arrives apologising for waiting in another church, All Saints: she confused the churches. She pleads with Troy in vain to name another wedding day.

COMMENT   It is fate that Fanny arrives too late for the wedding.

The gossiping female onlookers in the church injure Troy's male pride, so he is angry with Fanny.

Fanny is depicted as a victim of circumstance.

GLOSSARY   **quarter-jack** a mechanical man striking the quarter hours

CHAPTER 17

Note Hardy's use of biblical images (see Literary Terms).

At Casterbridge market Boldwood consciously observes Bathsheba's beauty, growing quickly jealous when he sees her with another farmer. Although Bathsheba notices the change in Boldwood, she values it as little as a 'wax fruit' (p. 169). She regrets the Valentine, but fears her apologies may be misunderstood.

COMMENT   Boldwood idealises Bathsheba; his jealousy augurs ill for the future.

Bathsheba is trapped by convention. An apology could either damage Boldwood's pride or make her appear forward.

GLOSSARY   **R.A.** a member of the Royal Academy of artists

CHAPTER 18

Boldwood falls in love. Boldwood paces restlessly in his stable-yard. A natural 'celibate' (p. 170), his feelings once roused are 'in extremity' (p. 171). He walks across a meadow towards Bathsheba's farm. Leaning on a gate, he observes Bathsheba with Gabriel, trying to make a ewe accept another lamb. Gabriel notices Bathsheba's embarrassment.

COMMENT   The description of spring harmonises with Boldwood's feelings.

Although Gabriel criticises Bathsheba's behaviour as 'coquettish' (p. 173), Hardy in his final comment exonerates her.

GLOSSARY   **Dryads** nymphs of the woods and forests
                        cabala secret plot

CHAPTER 19

Note how Hardy builds up tension. Bathsheba is out supervising the farm when Boldwood calls. He idolises her from a distance. Finally plucking up courage he seeks her out at work supervising the sheep-washing. As soon as they are alone he proposes, offering her a lady's life of leisure. **Ironically** (see Literary Terms) he declares that the Valentine gave him hope. Bathsheba, tense and guilty, apologises for the Valentine. She tells Boldwood she has 'not fallen in love' (p. 179) with him. Alarmed at his 'vehemence' (p. 180) and eager to escape, she pleads for time to consider.

COMMENT   It is **tragic irony** (see Literary Terms) that Bathsheba's
           Valentine has inspired such a strong passion in
           Boldwood. Her apologies come too late.

           The sheep washing-pool is both beautiful and essential
           for its purpose; Gabriel expertly immerses the sheep.

GLOSSARY   **Cyclops' eye** mythical creatures with only one eye each

A *Identify the speaker.*

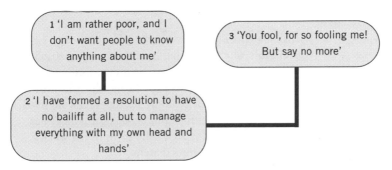

1 'I am rather poor, and I don't want people to know anything about me'

3 'You fool, for so fooling me! But say no more'

2 'I have formed a resolution to have no bailiff at all, but to manage everything with my own head and hands'

Identify the person 'to whom' this comment refers.

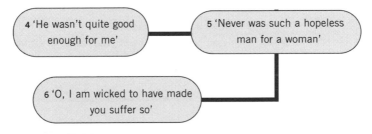

4 'He wasn't quite good enough for me'

5 'Never was such a hopeless man for a woman'

6 'O, I am wicked to have made you suffer so'

Check your answers on page 89.

 B *Consider these issues.*

a How Hardy changes the relationship of Gabriel and Bathsheba at Weatherbury.

b The purpose of the scene in Warren's Malthouse.

c How Fanny is portrayed in these chapters.

d How Hardy contrasts Bathsheba's reaction to Boldwood's proposal with her rejection of Gabriel's.

CHAPTERS 20–33: TROY'S COURTSHIP, BOLDWOOD'S REJECTION

CHAPTER 20

Hardy describes Bathsheba's thoughts. Bathsheba considers Boldwood's offer. Although he is very eligible, she prefers her independence as 'absolute mistress' (p. 181) of her farm. Next day, finding Gabriel in the barn grinding the sheep-shears, she asks him to deny rumours of a forthcoming marriage, but he refuses to lie. When she asks his opinion he pronounces her conduct 'unworthy' (p. 185). She gives him a week's notice, but he leaves immediately.

COMMENT   Bathsheba subconsciously values Gabriel's opinion.

Note the contrast between the calm Gabriel and his angry mistress.

GLOSSARY   **Ixion's punishment** he was tied eternally to a wheel of fire
Moses dismissed by Pharaoh, he showed the same dignity as Gabriel

CHAPTER 21

Note Hardy's use of another letter. Next day Bathsheba's sheep break a fence and get into the clover. They become bloated and in danger of dying. After one dies, Bathsheba sends a message ordering Gabriel to return. Gabriel refuses unless she asks him politely. Another sheep dies and Bathsheba writes a letter ending, 'Do not desert me, Gabriel!' (p. 191). Gabriel returns and, expertly lancing the sheep, saves it. A grateful Bathsheba asks him to stay on as shepherd.

COMMENT   It's fate that only Gabriel can save the sheep, so he is reinstated.

Bathsheba is torn between her pride and concern for her animals.

She exploits her femininity to make Gabriel return.

GLOSSARY   **store ewes** sheep kept for fattening

                      lettre-de-cachet a sealed letter requiring instant obedience

CHAPTER 22

Notice Hardy's description of the barn and the shearers.   Gabriel and the men work in the old barn. Bathsheba admires Gabriel's speed and skill. Boldwood enters and Gabriel is so preoccupied he accidentally wounds a ewe. Bathsheba reprimands him, then leaves with Boldwood. Gabriel quells the gossiping workmen, but secretly fears Bathsheba will marry Boldwood.

COMMENT   Hardy establishes the theme of rural tradition. 'Weatherbury was immutable' (p. 196) in comparison to life in the cities.

Note that some events are observed through Gabriel's eyes.

Gabriel wounds the ewe (see Sexual Symbolism).

GLOSSARY   **abraded** worn smooth with time

                     Guildenstern character in *Hamlet*

                     Aphrodite Greek goddess of love, born from the ocean

                     dam female sheep

                     hogs unshorn sheep

                     better wed over the mixen than over the moor (old village saying) it's better to marry a local villager than a foreigner

                     mixen a dunghill

CHAPTER 23

Note the visual beauty of the scene.   At the shearing supper Bathsheba sits at the head of the table in her house with the men outside. They eat drink and sing traditional ballads. Bathsheba also sings accompanied by Gabriel on flute and Boldwood singing bass. Afterwards Boldwood proposes again. Bathsheba says she will 'try to love' him (p. 210) and will give her answer by harvest time.

COMMENT   The social distance between Gabriel and Bathsheba is symbolised (see Literary Terms) by the seating arrangements and his exclusion from the house at the end of supper.

The ballad Bathsheba sings about a soldier with a 'winning tongue' (p. 208) is prophetic.

Bathsheba is flattered by Boldwood's adoration and wishes to 'make amends' (p. 211) for the Valentine.

GLOSSARY   **Chromis and Mnasylus** two young shepherds who make the drunk Silenus sing a long-winded ballad like Joseph's

CHAPTER 24

Consider your impressions of Troy.

After Boldwood leaves, Bathsheba goes out at night to check the farm buildings. Her skirt is caught on a strange soldier's spur. Troy remarks on her beauty as he tries to untangle her dress. Eventually Bathsheba frees herself. At home she questions Liddy for information about Troy.

COMMENT   The fickle Troy, last seen with Fanny, is now flattering Bathsheba.

Bathsheba is physically attracted to Troy. Hardy comments on her desire to be 'mastered' (p. 218) and Boldwood's failure to praise her beauty.

GLOSSARY   *genius loci* (Latin) spirit of the place
             gimp wired cord for trimming dresses
             the knot of knots marriage

CHAPTER 25

Hardy describes   Troy is attractive, articulate but 'common place
Troy's character. in action' (p. 220). He often lies to women. He is
better educated than the average soldier. Bathsheba
feels more relaxed because Boldwood is absent.
She is embarrassed when Troy helps with the
haymaking.

C OMMENT   Hardy's **authorial comments** (see Literary Terms)
presage unhappiness for Bathsheba with Troy.

GLOSSARY   **regrater** retailer
Corinthian a fashionable young man
passados forward fencing thrusts
cocks and windrows grass in haymaking was first raked into
rows (windrows) and then heaped up to dry (cocks)

CHAPTER 26

Notice how   Troy apologises for insulting Bathsheba. She
effectively Troy   unwillingly thanks him for offering to help with the
flatters Bathsheba.   haymaking. He flatters her so much, she becomes
'feverish' (p. 227). Troy tells her he will be leaving with
his regiment in a month's time. He protests that he fell
in love with her at first sight. Bathsheba denies this is
possible and asks the time, intending to go. Troy
attempts to give her his gold watch, an old family
heirloom. He extracts her permission to work in the
fields.

C OMMENT   At the beginning Troy's flattery is insincere. **Ironically**
(see Literary Terms) Bathsheba's spirited resistance
inspires real feeling. Troy acknowledges 'in setting a
gin, I have caught myself' (p. 231).

Bathsheba struggles to retain her dignity.

TROY'S COURTSHIP, BOLDWOOD'S REJECTION

GLOSSARY   **that Terrible Ten** the ten commandments
Tophet a heathen place of human sacrifices near Jerusalem
John Knox a strict Calvinist who lectured Mary Queen of
Scots

CHAPTER 27

Notice how Troy   Troy offers to help Bathsheba hive the bees. She dresses
breaks down   him in her veil, gloves and hat. When the bees are
Bathsheba's   hived, she removes the protective garments. She asks
defences.   him to show her the sword-exercise. He persuades her
to meet him alone that evening.

COMMENT   The hiving gives Troy and Bathsheba another
opportunity for physical contact.

Bathsheba quickly abandons the idea of taking Liddy as
a chaperone.

GLOSSARY   **costard, or quarrenden** types of apples

CHAPTER 28

Consider how the   Bathsheba waits for Troy at the secluded hollow. Troy
setting reflects   gives a fast display of cuts, lying that the sword is blunt.
Bathsheba's mood.   He cuts a lock of her hair and spits a caterpillar on her

breast, finally showing her the sword is sharp. She feels 'powerless' (p. 241), unable to prevent him kissing her before he leaves.

COMMENT   The sword is a **symbol** (see Literary Terms) of male virility. Troy's skill is impressive and dangerous.

Note the **images** (see Literary Terms) of light to describe the flashing blade. At the end of the chapter Hardy links both sword and man: Troy disappears 'in a flash like a brand' (p. 242).

Troy takes Bathsheba's hair as a trophy. Later we discover he has another lock from Fanny.

GLOSSARY   *Aurora militaris* dazzling military skill

Moses in Horeb the rock which Moses struck to produce abundant water was at Horeb (Exodus 17:6)

CHAPTER 29

Hardy contrasts   Gabriel realises Bathsheba is in love with Troy. He
Gabriel and Troy. reminds her of Boldwood's prior claims and criticises Troy, provoking Bathsheba to defend Troy. Gabriel responds by reaffirming his own faithful love, urging her not to trust Troy and advising more discretion. Bathsheba attempts to sack him again, but he refuses to leave unless she appoints a bailiff. He regards it his duty to stay and safeguard her 'concerns' (p. 249). She then withdraws her dismissal. Troy appears and Gabriel departs. On his way home he confirms his suspicion that Troy has lied to Bathsheba about attending church by a secret door.

COMMENT   Hardy presents the infatuated Bathsheba as naïve and blind.

He directly contrasts Troy and Gabriel on page 244. Gabriel acts as Bathsheba's conscience, reminding her of Boldwood's claims.

TROY'S COURTSHIP, BOLDWOOD'S REJECTION

Gabriel's warning to resist Troy 'before it is too late'
(p. 248) is prophetic.

GLOSSARY   **tything** division of land into tenths
                  Hippocrates an ancient Greek doctor

CHAPTER 30

Note Hardy's use   While Troy is away in Bath, Bathsheba writes
of another letter. Boldwood a letter declining his proposal of marriage.
                      She overhears her female servants discussing Troy and
                      leaps to his defence, throwing down the letter. Alone
                      with Liddy she confesses she loves Troy 'to very
                      distraction and misery and agony!' (p. 253). She
                      quarrels with Liddy when she fails to deny the rumours
                      of Troy's wildness. Finally Bathsheba apologises and
                      they are reconciled.

C OMMENT   Bathsheba contradicts herself, describing Troy as a
            'steady man in a wild way' (p. 254).

            Ironically Bathsheba speaks **melodramatically** (see
            Literary Terms) of dying in the Union or workhouse:
            this is Fanny's fate.

GLOSSARY   **Death's head** a human skull, **symbol** (see Literary Terms) of
                  mortality

CHAPTER 31

Note how Hardy   Bathsheba, on her way to visit Liddy, meets Boldwood
evokes sympathy   at sunset on Yalbury Hill. Boldwood entreats her to
for Bathsheba.   pity him and reproaches her for encouraging him with
                     the Valentine. Boldwood guesses the truth: Troy has
                     cheated him of Bathsheba. He threatens to kill Troy.
                     Bathsheba fears for Troy's safety.

C OMMENT   It is **tragic irony** (see Literary Terms) that Boldwood is
            plunged into savage jealousy of Troy.

Bathsheba is torn by guilt and pity for Boldwood, and by her love and concern for Troy.

GLOSSARY   **tergiversation** changing her mind

CHAPTER 32

Notice how Hardy creates tension and mystery. That night Maryann, left in charge at Bathsheba's house, sees someone stealing a horse and attaching it to a carriage. Gabriel, suspecting gypsies, borrows Boldwood's horses and gives chase with Coggan. They follow the horse's tracks and catch up with the 'thief' at Sherton turnpike, only to discover it is Bathsheba on her way to Bath. Gabriel counsels secrecy. Bathsheba has decided on impulse to drive to Bath to warn Troy about Boldwood and to renounce him.

COMMENT   Gabriel safeguards Bathsheba's reputation. She has acted unconventionally; in Coggan's words 'ladies don't drive at these hours' (p. 270).

Hardy comments on Bathsheba's self-deception. Once in her 'lover's arms' (p. 272) she is unlikely to renounce him.

GLOSSARY   **pinchbeck repeater** a watch made of cheap metal, which struck the hours

CHAPTER 33

Consider why Hardy included this scene. A week passes. Maryann receives a letter from Bathsheba explaining she is delayed on business. The workers are busy with the oat-harvest, assisted by the loyal Gabriel, when Cainy Ball brings news from Bath, where he has seen Bathsheba having a long discussion with Troy.

COMMENT   Maryann's story about the ominous broken key shows the strength of rural superstitions.

TROY'S COURTSHIP, BOLDWOOD'S REJECTION

The scene creates comedy and suspense: Cainy is impressed by the free hot spa water, while Gabriel is impatient for details about Bathsheba.

GLOSSARY   **Lammas** August, originally loaf mass or harvest festival
                  felon inflammation
                  bymeby by and by
                  stun-poll stupid head

A *Identify the speaker.*

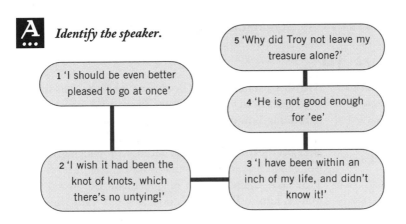

1 'I should be even better pleased to go at once'

2 'I wish it had been the knot of knots, which there's no untying!'

3 'I have been within an inch of my life, and didn't know it!'

4 'He is not good enough for 'ee'

5 'Why did Troy not leave my treasure alone?'

Identify the person 'to whom' this comment refers.

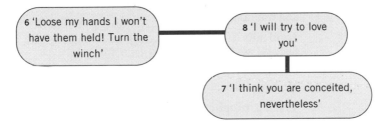

6 'Loose my hands I won't have them held! Turn the winch'

7 'I think you are conceited, nevertheless'

8 'I will try to love you'

Check your answers on page 89.

B *Consider these issues.*

a Hardy establishes the theme of rural tradition in these chapters from the sheep shearing to the oat-harvest.

b Troy's courtship of Bathsheba is partly presented through Gabriel's eyes as well as by Hardy as author.

c Bathsheba is attracted to Troy because of the elements of excitement, danger and romance in their encounters.

d Notice the effect on Boldwood of Bathsheba's rejection.

CHAPTERS 34–46: MARRIAGE AND SEPARATION

CHAPTER 34

Consider Troy's   Bathsheba refuses to see Boldwood when he calls to
treatment of   apologise. Boldwood confronts Troy in Weatherbury,
Boldwood.   reminding him of Fanny's claims, and offering him a
bribe to marry her. Troy appears to agree. However,
after overhearing Bathsheba address Troy lovingly,
Boldwood bribes Troy to marry Bathsheba instead.
Troy takes the ready cash in agreement. Boldwood
follows him to Bathsheba's house, where Troy slips a
newspaper cutting, announcing his marriage to
Bathsheba, through the bars of the door. Troy throws
out Boldwood's money; Boldwood vows revenge.

COMMENT   Troy makes a fool and an enemy of Boldwood by acting
and feigning agreement.

Ironically (see Literary Terms), he reveals his true
feelings for Fanny; he says that 'Miss Everdene
inflamed me, and displaced Fanny for a time' (p. 286).
He has searched in vain for Fanny.

There is **prophetic irony** (see Literary Terms) in
Boldwood's threat to kill Troy.

GLOSSARY   **surrogate's** the bishop's representative, who supplied the
marriage licence
Shade in the Mournful Fields by Acheron a ghost of the dead near
the river of Acheron in the Underworld

CHAPTER 35

Notice how Hardy   Next morning Troy throws down money to Coggan
contrasts Troy   and Gabriel from Bathsheba's bedroom window to
with the   drink his health. Gabriel leaves the money, rejecting
unsuccessful   Coggan's advice to flatter their new master. Boldwood
suitors.   appears on horseback, tense and silent.

COMMENT   Hardy uses a framing **device** (see Literary Terms) to
           emphasise Troy's arrogance.

           Boldwood's appearance creates an atmosphere of
           foreboding.

CHAPTER 36

Consider how   On the night of the harvest supper, Troy ignores
Hardy builds up   Gabriel's warning of bad weather. Having purchased his
tension.   discharge from the army, he is now master of the farm.
                    Despite Bathsheba's protests, he orders strong drink for
                    the men to celebrate his marriage and sends all the
                    women and children home. Bathsheba and then
                    Gabriel leave soon afterwards. Gabriel, observing more
                    ominous weather signs, decides to cover the ricks. He
                    discovers the men unconscious in the barn. Single-
                    handed he covers the wheat with waterproof cloths and
                    then starts to thatch the barley ricks.

COMMENT   By marrying Troy Bathsheba has lost control of the
           farm. At the time in which the novel is set, the property
           of a woman, on marriage, automatically became her
           husband's.

           Hardy contrasts the shrewd, farsighted Gabriel with the
           feckless Troy.

           Gabriel, knowing the exact financial value of each rick,
           seeks to serve Bathsheba faithfully.

           The wedding feast is a **parody** (see Literary Terms) of
           the sheep-shearing feast.

GLOSSARY   **Saint Vitus's dances** jerky movements caused by illness
           ath'art across
           palimpsest a paper or parchment written on twice, with the
             original text faintly visible
           thatching beetle kind of mallet
           rick-stick and spars thatching tools

MARRIAGE AND SEPARATION

CHAPTER 37

Notice how Hardy describes the storm.   Gabriel works on thatching despite the thunder and lightning. Bathsheba arrives and helps by carrying reeds up the ladder. When lightning strikes a nearby tree, Gabriel urges Bathsheba to leave. Gabriel checks that the men are still unconscious in the barn. Bathsheba confides in Gabriel the reasons for her hasty marriage. Finally she agrees to go inside.

COMMENT   Bathsheba values Gabriel's good opinion. She agreed to marry Troy, fearing scandal and desertion.

Gabriel risks his life to save the crops.

GLOSSARY   **Hinnom** valley near Jerusalem associated with heathen worship

zephyr gentle breeze

CHAPTER 38

Gabriel works all night. The rain starts as Gabriel thatches the last rick. At dawn journeying home *Note the changes in Boldwood's character.* Gabriel meets Boldwood. He is shocked to discover all Boldwood's ricks were uncovered and damaged. Boldwood is indifferent to his losses and confides in Gabriel his disappointed hopes of Bathsheba. He excuses Bathsheba from blame and talks of suicide.

COMMENT   Gabriel sees the **irony** (see Literary Terms) of his situation: eight months earlier (Chapter 6) he saved Bathsheba's crops from fire.

Boldwood seems unbalanced and depressed, and like Bathsheba he confides in Gabriel.

GLOSSARY   **Mercury** messenger of the gods, here depicted in Flaxman's painting leading the suitors in the *Odyssey* to the Underworld

CHAPTER 39

Troy leads the gig in which Bathsheba is seated up Yalbury Hill one evening. He has lost over £100 betting on the races, and they quarrel when Troy refuses to give up his plans to attend another race meeting. A woman (Fanny) appears toiling up the hill; she asks the way to Casterbridge workhouse. Fanny recognises Troy and faints. When Bathsheba attempts to help her, Troy orders Bathsheba to lead the horse on up the hill. Alone with Fanny Troy gives her all his money and arranges to meet her on Grey's Bridge next morning.

Consider the timing of Fanny's reappearance.

Troy refuses to answer Bathsheba's questions about the woman's identity.

COMMENT It is fate that Troy, having fruitlessly searched for Fanny, should re-encounter her now that he's married to Bathsheba.

There is a sharp contrast between Troy's solicitude for Fanny and his careless disregard of Bathsheba's wishes.

Troy has confirmed Gabriel's fears and is gambling away the profits of the farm.

The remote setting makes Fanny appear more vulnerable. Her destination, the workhouse, was the refuge of the destitute in Victorian times.

CHAPTER 40

Think about why Hardy describes Fanny's journey in such detail.

Fanny walks on, only stopping to sleep for a few hours. She uses two sticks as crutches. Near Casterbridge she can only continue by leaning on a large dog. Finally she collapses on the workhouse steps and is carried inside.

COMMENT Fanny is presented as a small weak figure in a dark hostile landscape.

Hardy evokes the reader's sympathy. Fanny's fear that she will never see Troy again – 'Perhaps I shall be in my grave' (p. 322) – is **prophetically ironic** (see Literary Terms).

GLOSSARY   **Jacquet Droz** a designer of clockwork human figures

Juggernaut (Indian legend) a huge remorseless force

CHAPTER 41

Troy extorts £20 from Bathsheba, who assumes the money is for betting. When Troy opens his watch Bathsheba notices a blonde lock of hair. Troy tells her the hair belonged to a former sweetheart; he refuses to burn it, ignoring Bathsheba's entreaties. Troy confirms Bathsheba's suspicions that the woman they met on Yalbury Hill is the sweetheart.

Hardy shows us Bathsheba's thoughts.

Next morning Troy departs for Casterbridge without informing Bathsheba. When Bathsheba learns that Fanny has died in the workhouse she orders Joseph Poorgrass to fetch the coffin for burial at Weatherbury. Bathsheba strongly suspects that Fanny was Troy's former sweetheart. Later Bathsheba questions Liddy, discovering that Fanny had blonde hair and a lover in Troy's regiment, similar to Troy in appearance. She concludes that Fanny was Troy's sweetheart.

COMMENT

Troy and Bathsheba's quarrels **ironically** (see Literary Terms) prove the truth of Troy's remark: 'All romances end at marriage' (p. 350).

Bathsheba still loves Troy, but she is now aware of his faults. Her feelings for Gabriel are changing to the 'genuine friendship of a sister' (p. 334). Despite regretting her lost independence, she sometimes imagines alternative marriages to Gabriel and Boldwood.

Both Gabriel and Joseph try to prevent Bathsheba from learning the truth about Fanny and Troy.

GLOSSARY   **non lucendo principles** contrary ideas
                        Diana goddess of chastity and the moon
                        neshness tenderness
                        limber pliant, fragile
                        hent hint

CHAPTER 42

Note how Hardy creates a ghostly atmosphere. Joseph collects Fanny's coffin from the workhouse. He drives into thick fog and stops at the Buck's Head inn, where he meets Coggan and Clark. He gets so drunk he forgets the time. Gabriel arrives and drives the coffin back to Weatherbury. The funeral is postponed to the following day. Against Gabriel's advice Bathsheba insists that the coffin be brought into her house that night. Gabriel removes the words 'and child' (p. 351) from the coffin-lid.

COMMENT   Hardy **juxtaposes** (see Literary Terms) the tragic death of Fanny with the earthy drunken wisdom of the workmen.

Boldwood and Gabriel both conceal the identity of Fanny's lover from the villagers. Gabriel also tries to shield Bathsheba from learning about the illegitimate baby.

GLOSSARY   **grim Leveller** death
                        dew-bit breakfast taken in the field
                        horning wildness, like a frisky horse

CHAPTER 43

Liddy whispers to Bathsheba the rumour of the illegitimate child, and Bathsheba recalls the meeting on

Think why the chapter is entitled 'Fanny's Revenge'. Yalbury Hill. Longing to confide in Gabriel, she goes to his cottage and observes him through the window praying, but she changes her mind and does not call. Back at the house Bathsheba opens the coffin and sees for herself the baby lying beside Fanny, confirming her suspicions that Fanny was Troy's sweetheart. She assuages her jealousy by placing flowers around Fanny's head. Troy returns and learns about the baby. He kneels and kisses Fanny, but he refuses to kiss Bathsheba. Bathsheba runs away.

COMMENT Bathsheba values Gabriel's Christian stoical attitude. He views 'the horizon of circumstances' objectively 'without any special regard to his own standpoint' (p. 355).

Troy's tender love for Fanny is contrasted to his cruel rejection of Bathsheba, his wife. He regards Fanny now as his 'very wife!' (p. 361).

Bathsheba sees both herself and Fanny as 'victims' (p. 361).

GLOSSARY **Vashti** the beautiful wife of the King of Persia, replaced by Esther

Mosaic law in the Old Testament – the law of Moses – the law of revenge

CHAPTER 44

Notice how the   Bathsheba sleeps outdoors and awakes to find she
setting reflects   is near a swamp. Liddy informs her that Troy has
Bathsheba's mood.   left the house. Bathsheba only returns to the house
                         after Fanny's coffin has been removed for burial.
                         Bathsheba and Liddy spend the day encamped in a
                         disused attic, but Troy fails to return. At sunset they
                         observe men erecting an ornate tombstone in the
                         churchyard.

COMMENT   Bathsheba decides not to run away but 'stand her
                 ground' (p. 366). She wishes to retain her pride and
                 social position.

                 The chapter ends mysteriously with Troy absent
                 and Liddy failing to discover who the tombstone
                 is for.

GLOSSARY   **cut to pieces** Bathsheba **ironically** (see Literary Terms) recalls
                 Troy's own words in the sword exercise (Chapter 28)
                 stump bedstead a bed with the posts cut down

CHAPTER 45

Consider the   After Bathsheba leaves, Troy re-covers the coffin. He
changes in Troy's   lies awake recalling the events of the previous day when
character.   he waited in vain for Fanny in Casterbridge, then went
                        to the races and finally returning home found
                        Bathsheba with the coffin.

                        In Casterbridge he purchases the most ornate
                        tombstone he can afford with a special inscription,
                        insisting on delivery that day. On his return to
                        Weatherbury he plants flowers on Fanny's grave. He
                        shelters from the rain in the church porch, where he
                        sleeps that night.

COMMENT   Troy's concern for Fanny is superseded by his self-
                absorption; he is angry when Fanny fails to arrive at

Grey's Bridge, recalling a similar muddle on their abortive wedding day.

Fanny's grave is in an 'obscure' (p. 372) part of the churchyard, because she was a pauper with an illegitimate baby.

Hardy comments critically on the 'futility' of Troy's 'romantic doings' which arise from guilt and contain an 'element of absurdity' (p. 373).

GLOSSARY   **crocketed** ornamented with leaf shapes
                     flying crumbling or eroding

CHAPTER 46

Notice how Hardy uses weather as a fatal force. The rain worsens and the spouting gargoyle over Fanny's grave washes away the flowers. When Troy wakes he is so depressed he leaves without clearing up the damage.

Bathsheba learns that Troy has been seen on the Budmouth road. In the churchyard she reads the inscription on the tombstone and asks Gabriel to replace the earth and orders that the lead work on the gargoyle be redirected. She replants the flowers and wipes away the mud from the tombstone.

COMMENT Hardy emphasises the obscurity of Fanny's grave, the place where sinners and outcasts are buried.

It is fate that Troy's efforts at reparation are undone by the rain.

Bathsheba, in contrast to Troy, repairs the damage. She ceases to be jealous, cleaning the loving inscription in Fanny's memory.

GLOSSARY   **Ruysdael and Hobbema** two Dutch landscape artists

A Identify the speaker.

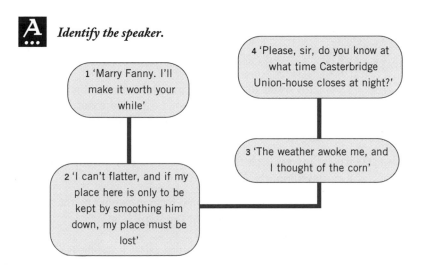

1 'Marry Fanny. I'll make it worth your while'

2 'I can't flatter, and if my place here is only to be kept by smoothing him down, my place must be lost'

3 'The weather awoke me, and I thought of the corn'

4 'Please, sir, do you know at what time Casterbridge Union-house closes at night?'

Identify the person 'to whom' this comment refers.

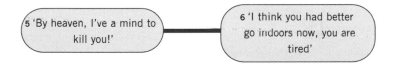

5 'By heaven, I've a mind to kill you!'

6 'I think you had better go indoors now, you are tired'

Check your answers on page 89.

B Consider these issues.

a Notice the deterioration of Boldwood's character, a source of future danger.

b Bathsheba's attitude to Gabriel is changing. Make notes on any evidence and reasons you find to support this change.

c Plot Fanny's last days, her death and burial. Think about how far these events contribute to the breakdown of Troy and Bathsheba's marriage.

d Examine Hardy's use of weather as a force controlling events in these chapters.

CHAPTERS 47–57: ENDINGS

CHAPTER 47

Notice the description of the weather and landscape.

Troy walks to Lulwind Cove and swims in the bay. Carried out to sea by a strong current, he treads water until he attracts the attention of a ship's boat and is rescued.

COMMENT   Troy vanishes from Bathsheba's life as quickly and mysteriously as he entered it.

It is fate that he is rescued from drowning by the opportune appearance of the ship's boat.

GLOSSARY   **Balboa** Spanish explorer, the first person to see the Pacific Ocean
pillars of Hercules the classical name for the entrance to the Mediterranean
en papillon butterfly stroke

CHAPTER 48

Consider Bathsheba's reaction to the news of Troy's death.

Bathsheba believes Troy will return and she foresees ruin and eviction from the farm. The following Saturday in Casterbridge, a stranger informs her that Troy has drowned. When she faints with shock, Boldwood catches her and carries her into the King's Arms inn. Recovering, she questions the stranger and drives herself home. Her instinctive belief that Troy is alive is shaken by an eye-witness account in a newspaper and by the arrival of Troy's clothes, which were found by the coastguard. She restrains her impulse to burn the lock of Fanny's hair in Troy's watch, keeping it in her memory.

COMMENT   Boldwood has his moment of triumph when he supports Bathsheba; his hopes are renewed 'his face

flushed with the suppressed excitement of an
unutterable thought' (p. 387).

Ironically (see Literary Terms) Bathsheba is 'perfectly
convinced' that Troy 'is still alive' (p. 388), yet the
circumstantial evidence proves death.

GLOSSARY   **phaeton** an open four-wheeled carriage for a pair of horses

CHAPTER 49

Note Gabriel's rise   Bathsheba finally appoints Gabriel as bailiff.
and Boldwood's   Boldwood's crops rot and Gabriel accepts the
decline.   stewardship of Boldwood's farm too for a small share of
                          the profits. The villagers respect Gabriel as a prosperous
                          successful man. Bathsheba assumes mourning, arousing
                          Boldwood's wild hopes. She returns to Norcombe to
                          stay with her aunt for two months. Boldwood, on
                          questioning Liddy, learns that Bathsheba has
                          mentioned the possibility of marriage in six years' time
                          if Troy fails to return. He becomes obsessed with the
                          idea that his fidelity will be rewarded.

COMMENT   Gabriel is a prudent businessman, insisting on a share
                 of Boldwood's profits.

                 Although Gabriel buys new clothes, he is thrifty at
                 home, a direct contrast to Troy.

                 Ironically (see Literary Terms), Bathsheba still retains
                 the belief that Troy is alive and wears mourning with
                 reluctance.

                 Boldwood shows increasing signs of mental
                 disturbance.

GLOSSARY   **Rachel** the woman Jacob loved; he had to work fourteen years
                  for her father Laban before he gained permission to marry
                  her

ENDINGS

CHAPTER 50

Gabriel takes Bathsheba's and Boldwood's sheep to sell at Greenhill Fair, where Troy is the star performer in a travelling circus. Troy, recognising Bathsheba in a reserved seat, stipulates that he will only perform silently. Although he adds extra make-up, he realises that Pennyways, Bathsheba's sacked bailiff, has recognised him. After the performance, Troy, disguised with a heavy beard, searches for Pennyways in the refreshment tent. Hearing Bathsheba's voice, he cuts a peephole to spy on her with Boldwood. Pennyways enters and when Bathsheba refuses to speak to him, he

Hardy uses a note as writes a note informing her of Troy's presence. Troy *a plot device (see* quickly steals the note before Bathsheba can read it, and *Literary Terms).* runs away. He finds Pennyways and speaks to him privately.

COMMENT   Hardy describes the busy atmosphere of the fair and adds humour with the workmen's comments on the circus performance.

We learn about Troy's history after his disappearance at Lulwind Cove. He is undecided whether to reclaim Bathsheba, fearing her scorn.

Note Troy's enjoyment of risks and disguise, also his ability to act quickly under pressure.

GLOSSARY   **Nijni Novgorod** Soviet city where a huge fair was held
Turpin's ride ... Black Bess a play about a notorious highwayman Turpin and his horse
Tom King Turpin's partner in crime
penetralia innermost part, the holiest place in a temple

CHAPTER 51

Notice the changes in Bathsheba's character.

Boldwood on horseback accompanies Bathsheba when she returns to Weatherbury. He proposes marriage again. He counters Bathsheba's belief that Troy is alive by stating that if Troy does not return in six years she is legally entitled to remarry. Bathsheba gives her word not to marry anyone else, but postpones a final answer until Christmas. Bathsheba confides her predicament and fears for Boldwood's sanity to Gabriel, who advises her to give a conditional promise.

COMMENT

Bathsheba acts maturely; she greatly regrets sending the fatal Valentine and feels bound in conscience to consider Boldwood's proposal seriously.

Boldwood displays insensitivity: aware that Bathsheba does not love him, he still uses emotional blackmail to exploit her guilt over the Valentine.

Significantly, Bathsheba regards Gabriel as an arbiter on 'morals' (p. 417), yet she is piqued that he does not ask her to marry him again.

CHAPTER 52

Consider the purpose of the many short scenes.

At Christmas Boldwood holds a large party. Bathsheba is very reluctant to go and deliberately wears mourning, whereas Boldwood dresses in a new coat. Boldwood confides his hopes to Gabriel, who warns him against disappointment. At Casterbridge Troy, after questioning Pennyways for news of Bathsheba, decides to gatecrash the party and reclaim his wife. Boldwood offers Gabriel a larger share in the farm in recompense for his unrequited love of Bathsheba. Gabriel again tries to calm Boldwood. Boldwood puts the engagement ring he has bought in his pocket in readiness. At Casterbridge Troy disguised in an overcoat sets off for Weatherbury.

ENDINGS

COMMENT   Boldwood's wild hopes are contrasted with the sober
warnings of Gabriel. Boldwood is generous towards his
disappointed rival.

Bathsheba now distrusts her beauty and its power,
fearing its effect on Boldwood (see Chapter 1 for the
contrast).

Troy, inflamed by Pennyways's sensual description
of Bathsheba and tired of his freedom as a 'needy
adventurer', decides to reclaim Bathsheba. He assumes
yet another disguise.

GLOSSARY   **Shadrach, Meshach and Abednego** Daniel's companions in the
Bible who emerged unharmed from a fire
ayless alias
lammocken lounging, loitering
scram insignificant mean
plimmed swelled
scroff kindling
Juno goddess, special protectress of marriage and women
Noachian of the time of Noah, old fashioned

CHAPTER 53

Notice the   Outside Boldwood's house, the villagers discuss the
importance of the   rumour that Troy is alive. When Troy is seen outside
timing of events.   Warren's Malthouse, Laban is sent to warn Bathsheba.
She refuses to dance and after an hour attempts to
leave. Boldwood presses his suit and extracts her
promise to marry him in six years' time. Alarmed at
his vehemence she agrees to wear the engagement
ring that evening. Just as Laban is about to warn
Bathsheba, Troy appears and she recognises him. She
fails to react to Troy's orders, so he seizes her roughly,
making her scream. Boldwood shoots Troy. Then
prevented from shooting himself, he rushes out of the
house.

COMMENT   Hardy skilfully builds the tension to a dramatic climax.

Bathsheba is mainly passive; she is bullied by both
Boldwood and Troy.

It is fate that the villagers fail to warn Bathsheba in
time.

Hardy has prepared the reader for Boldwood's
murderous jealousy. He has been cheated of Bathsheba
twice by Troy (see Chapter 31).

GLOSSARY   *Concurritur – Horae Momento* (Horace's *Satires*, Book 1) battle is
               joined in a moment in time
               to ho to pine
               thik that
               gutta serena blindness in the optic nerve

CHAPTER 54

Note the more   Boldwood surrenders himself at Casterbridge gaol.
tragic (see Literary Bathsheba cradles the dead Troy on her lap and sends
Terms) tone of the Gabriel to fetch a surgeon. Then she has Troy's body
story.   moved to her house where she prepares it for burial.
                     When the surgeon arrives he is angry that the body has
                     been moved – there will be an inquest. He ministers to
                     Bathsheba who has 'a series of fainting fits' (p. 443).

ENDINGS

COMMENT   The pace of events quickens in the aftermath of the
           shooting.

           Bathsheba reacts with courage and dignity to Troy's
           death. When she collapses she blames herself for the
           murder.

GLOSSARY   **Melpomene** the Muse of Tragedy, daughter of Zeus
           stoic a follower of an Athenian philosophy, which believed in
           showing indifference to both pleasure and pain

CHAPTER 55

Consider the role   The following March the workmen see the court
of the workmen.   officials driving towards Casterbridge for Boldwood's
           trial. There is a plea for mercy on the grounds of
           insanity; an entire trousseau has been discovered
           locked away in Boldwood's house. However, Boldwood
           pleads guilty and is sentenced to death. The night
           before the execution the scaffold is prepared and
           Gabriel spends two hours with Boldwood. A reprieve
           arrives; Boldwood's sentence is changed to life
           imprisonment.

COMMENT   Hardy covers large areas of time fast.

           Boldwood's carefully labelled acquisitions for Bathsheba
           evoke pathos and are evidence of mental derangement.

           Hardy creates suspense with the last-minute reprieve.

           Bathsheba is depressed and much more reliant on
           Gabriel.

GLOSSARY   **javelin-men** medieval pike men who protected the judges
           Decalogue the Ten Commandments

CHAPTER 56

Notice Bathsheba's Bathsheba's health slowly improves, but she becomes a
increasing recluse, leaving most of the farm management to
dependence on Gabriel. On her first excursion to Weatherbury
Gabriel. churchyard she views the extra inscription she ordered
to go on Fanny's tombstone in remembrance of Troy.
She meets Gabriel on his way to choir practice. He tells
her of his decision to emigrate, despite being offered
the lease of Boldwood's farm. She pleads with him to
stay.

Note Hardy uses Soon after the anniversary of Troy's death, Gabriel
another letter as a writes a formal letter of resignation. Bathsheba calls on
plot device (see Gabriel that evening. He tells her that he has now
Literary Terms). decided to take Boldwood's farm, but he wants to
resign his position as Bathsheba's bailiff, because there
are rumours that he intends to marry her. Bathsheba
gives Gabriel the confidence to propose again. She
accepts quickly and as he escorts her home they mainly
discuss farming matters.

COMMENT   Ironically (see Literary Terms) when Bathsheba calls
on Gabriel (a contrast to Chapter 43 when she changed
her mind) to plead her need and dependence on
Gabriel, she actually initiates the proposal. She herself
says 'it seems exactly as if I had come courting you'
(p. 458).

Hardy contrasts the romance of Troy's courtship
with Bathsheba and Gabriel's 'substantial affection'
(p. 458).

GLOSSARY   **all a-sheenan ... o'handlen** a poem by William Barnes
floods drown from the Songs of Solomon

CHAPTER 57

A happy ending. Bathsheba and Gabriel are married quietly and secretly at Bathsheba's insistence, with Liddy and Laban the only witnesses. News of the marriage spreads. That evening the village band plays outside their house and Gabriel sends food and drink to Warren's Malthouse for them to celebrate.

COMMENT Bathsheba is more serious and nervous. 'She never laughed readily now' (p. 465).

The villagers provide a comic perspective. They quickly accept Gabriel's rise in status, whereas they remained distant and critical of Troy. Gabriel's proprietorial term 'my wife' (p. 464) is gently mocked and Joseph Poorgrass has the last grudging word of approval.

A Identify the speaker.

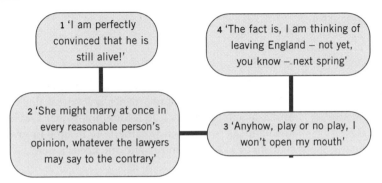

1 'I am perfectly convinced that he is still alive!'

4 'The fact is, I am thinking of leaving England – not yet, you know – next spring'

2 'She might marry at once in every reasonable person's opinion, whatever the lawyers may say to the contrary'

3 'Anyhow, play or no play, I won't open my mouth'

Identify the person 'to whom' this comment refers.

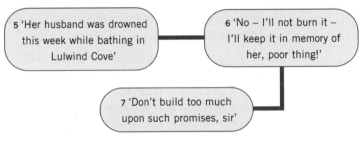

5 'Her husband was drowned this week while bathing in Lulwind Cove'

6 'No – I'll not burn it – I'll keep it in memory of her, poor thing!'

7 'Don't build too much upon such promises, sir'

Check your answers on page 89.

B Consider these issues.

a How Hardy charts the rise of Gabriel in contrast to the decline of Boldwood.

b Hardy builds up tension and suspense in Chapters 52 and 53.

c The plot relies heavily on coincidences in the final section, particularly in relation to Troy.

d Hardy contrasts Boldwood's protracted courtship with the swiftness and ease of Bathsheba and Gabriel's marriage.

PART THREE

COMMENTARY

THEMES

FATE

Fate and coincidence are used frequently in the plot.

Bathsheba arrives in time to prevent Gabriel suffocating in his lambing hut. Gabriel tragically loses his flock over a precipice. In his search for employment Gabriel just happens to arrive in Weatherbury in time to save Bathsheba's crops from fire and she needs a new shepherd.

Bathsheba's Valentine sent as a joke has a fatal effect on Boldwood, who falls desperately in love with her. Boldwood reads Fanny's letter intended only for Gabriel. It is fate that Fanny confuses two churches so Troy does not marry her.

Bathsheba is forced to withdraw her dismissal of Gabriel, when the following day her sheep become fatally sick and only Gabriel has the requisite skill to cure them. It is fate that on the night of the shearing supper when Boldwood is given hope that Bathsheba may accept his proposal by harvest time, she first meets Troy. In the intervening time she becomes infatuated with Troy.

Notice the role of fate in the disintegration of Bathsheba and Troy's marriage.

Although Troy has searched hard for Fanny, he re-encounters her when it is too late on Yalbury Hill and he's married Bathsheba. His sentimental preservation of Fanny's hair causes a serious quarrel and gives Bathsheba a valuable clue to her identity. It is fate that, due to Joseph's drunkenness, the funeral is postponed, providing Bathsheba with the opportunity to open the coffin and discover Fanny with her dead baby.

The weather becomes a malignant force, an agent of fate in the later parts of the story. The storm at Harvest supper nearly destroys Bathsheba's crops. Rain washes away the flowers that Troy has carefully planted on Fanny's grave.

Hardy relies heavily on coincidence in the final stages of the plot.

By chance Troy is saved from drowning, although circumstantial evidence suggests death. Luckily Troy arrives at the refreshment tent at Greenhill Fair in time to intercept Pennyways's note, thus keeping his presence a secret from Bathsheba. It is fate that on the very night Bathsheba agrees to marry Boldwood, Troy returns and Boldwood shoots him.

LOVE

Hardy compares Bathsheba's three suitors.

Hardy contrasts both the romantic love of Troy and the obsessive passion of Boldwood with the 'camaraderie' (p. 458) of Bathsheba and Gabriel's final union.

The penniless Bathsheba rejects Gabriel's first proposal, as she does not love him. She sensibly advises him to 'marry a woman with money, who would stock a larger farm for you' (p. 81). As a wealthy gentleman farmer Boldwood offers Bathsheba a rise in social status, but he too is rejected, as she does not love him.

Although Bathsheba quickly falls in love with Troy, Hardy presents this infatuation, based on sexual attraction, as superficial and unstable. Troy deserts Fanny and once married to Bathsheba treats her carelessly, proving his own words 'All romances end at marriage' (p. 330).

By the end of the novel Bathsheba and Gabriel's love has gradually grown from a long working partnership, friendship and mutual respect. They are aware of each

other's 'rougher sides' or faults; their 'romance growing
up in the interstices of a mass of hard prosaic reality'
(p. 458).

FARMING & COMMERCE

Hardy shows the events of the farming year – lambing,
sheep shearing and harvest. The natural settings are
both beautiful and described precisely. We see
Bathsheba trading in the old cornmarket and the sheep
shearing in the great barn where 'the barn was natural
to the shearers, and the shearers were in harmony with
the barn' (p. 196).

Gabriel, as hero,
prospers in his
farming and rises
in social status.

Gabriel is a caring and skilled shepherd, but he is also a
businessman. At the start of the novel he has worked
hard and progressed from shepherd to bailiff to leasing
his own farm. When he loses his sheep he becomes a
shepherd again, working for Bathsheba. Later he
becomes Bathsheba's bailiff and manages Boldwood's
farm with a share of the profits, riding daily over 'two
thousand acres' (p. 391). After Boldwood's
imprisonment he is offered the tenancy of Boldwood's
farm. By the time he marries Bathsheba he has become
her equal.

A FEMINIST PERSPECTIVE OF THE THEMES

All the suitors regard Bathsheba as a valuable object.
- Bathsheba rejects Gabriel's first proposal because she
  'hates to be thought men's property' (p. 78)
- Boldwood accuses Troy of stealing his 'treasure'
  (p. 261)
- After Troy marries Bathsheba, he becomes master of
  her farm 'ruling now in the room of his wife' (p. 297)
  and gambling away the profits
- Troy describes Bathsheba as a 'dashing piece of
  womanhood, Juno-wife of mine' (p. 423)

Notice how
Bathsheba seriously
jeopardises her
position when she
marries Troy.

- Neither Gabriel nor Troy has faith in Bathsheba's powers to maintain the farm. Gabriel insists she needs a bailiff and blames her 'instability' (p. 301) for the failure to cover the ricks. This is an unjust charge: Troy ignored Gabriel's weather warnings while Bathsheba braved the storm to help Gabriel thatch the ricks. At Greenhill Fair Troy decides against returning to Bathsheba, because he fears she will fail at her farming and he will become 'liable for her maintenance' (p. 400)
- Later Troy changes his mind, assuming the right to reclaim Bathsheba, because she has 'plenty of money, and a house and farm, and horses, and comfort' (p. 427)
- **Ironically** (see Literary Terms), Bathsheba herself fears that if Troy returns 'the days of their tenancy of the Upper Farm would be numbered' (p. 385). The trustees accepted Bathsheba as tenant after her uncle died. She worries about the 'legal effects of her marriage' on her 'position' (p. 385)

Hardy set the novel before the 1870 Married Women's Property Act was passed, which allowed women to retain and acquire property independently of their husbands.

STRUCTURE

Hardy interweaves Fanny and Troy's story with the main plot. He uses a parallel structure for Boldwood's courtship of Bathsheba. Troy cheats Boldwood twice, once before harvest and at the fatal Christmas party.

The fact that the novel was written as a serial for the *Cornhill Magazine* affects the structure: Hardy often leaves the reader in suspense and builds up tension to dramatic climaxes (see Chapters 52 and 53).

Chapter 2

Has risen from being a shepherd and then a bailiff to an independent farmer leasing 'the small sheep-farm of which Norcombe Hill was a portion' and stocking it 'with two hundred sheep'
(p. 59)

Chapter 5

Is ruined: his uninsured sheep are killed over a precipice. After selling everything to pay his debts he is 'a free man with the clothes he stood up in, and nothing more'
(p. 87)

GABRIEL OAK'S RISE AND FALL...

Chapter 6

Fails to be hired as either bailiff or shepherd at Casterbridge hiring fair

Chapter 7

Is hired by Bathsheba as her shepherd after he has saved her ricks from fire
(p. 98)

N
A
D
I
R

ZENITH

Chapter 57

Marries Bathsheba as her equal; takes over the management of both farms

...AND RISE

Chapter 56

Is offered the lease of Boldwood's farm after his imprisonment but decides to emigrate to California.
(p. 453)
Soon afterwards he changes his mind, resigning as Bathsheba's bailiff and making arrangements to take over 'Little Weatherbury Farm... at Lady-day'
(p. 456)

Chapter 49

Is finally appointed as Bathsheba's bailiff a 'long delayed installation'. Also manages Boldwood's farm with a small share of the profits. Rides daily over 'two thousand acres'
(pp. 390-1)

FRAMINGS

Hardy links plot and setting, using windows and doorways to reveal character. Fanny's weak position is emphasised by her gazing up at Troy, framed in a window of his barracks. Boldwood's entrance at Warren's Malthouse casts a gloom 'a shade darkened the door' (p. 160). At the shearing supper Bathsheba as mistress sits at the head of the table inside her house, while the workmen sit outside. Troy locks Boldwood safely outside the door of Bathsheba's house before handing him the newspaper cutting about his marriage to Bathsheba. Next morning Troy throws down money from an upper window in patronising fashion for Gabriel and Coggan to drink his health. Bathsheba, worrying about Fanny, watches Gabriel at prayer through his cottage window afraid to disturb him. In a parallel scene at the end of the novel, she overcomes her fear of impropriety and knocks on the door.

LETTERS

Letters are used to advance the plot and reveal character.
- Bathsheba sends Boldwood a Valentine with dramatic and unexpected effects. The 'red seal became as a blot of blood on the retina of his eye' (p. 149), portending both passion and bloodshed
- **Ironically** (see Literary Terms), Gabriel ignores Fanny's request for secrecy and shows her letter about her forthcoming marriage to Boldwood
- Bathsheba writes a letter ending 'Do not desert me, Gabriel' (p. 191) to induce the 'love-led' shepherd to return and tend to her sick sheep
- Bathsheba writes a letter rejecting Boldwood, but is later forced to hear his bitter reproaches at Yalbury Hill

• Gabriel's formal letter of resignation acts as a catalyst for his second successful proposal

BALANCE OF CHARACTERS

The characters are viewed in different relationships; their personalities form contrasts. The passive Fanny contrasts with the spirited Bathsheba. The superficially attractive Troy is a foil for both the solid dependable Gabriel and the brooding intense Boldwood.

CHARACTERS

BATHSHEBA EVERDENE

Bathsheba is first portrayed as a poor, attractive cottage girl admiring her reflection in a mirror. Although well educated she is 'too wild' (p. 76) to be a governess, suggesting she will behave unpredictably. She quickly rejects Gabriel's proposal, preferring her independence.

She acts bravely in a crisis, saving Gabriel from suffocation (Chapter 3). Later she shows courage helping Gabriel in the storm and preparing Troy's corpse for burial. Admired for her 'cleverness' (p. 384) by the trustees of Weatherbury farm, she is appointed mistress after her uncle dies. She adapts well, becoming a 'supervising and cool woman' (p. 99) and takes the unconventional step of managing the farm herself without a bailiff. She wins the loyalty of her workmen by giving them a bonus and acts responsibly in sending men to search for Fanny. As the only woman in the cornmarket she enjoys the admiration of all the other farmers except Boldwood.

Dark and
attractive
Lively and
unconventional
Independent and
volatile
Brave

She sends Boldwood the Valentine as a joke. When he proposes, although she does not love him, she postpones her answer because of her feelings of guilt

about the intense passion she has provoked. She
confides in Gabriel, the first of several occasions, but is
so offended by his criticism that she sacks him. She is
forced to retract the dismissal after he saves her sheep.

By a twist of fate on the very night she gives Boldwood
hope of a favourable answer she meets Troy. The
romance and danger of their meetings thrill her. She
rejects Boldwood despite her guilt and impulsively
drives to Bath to warn Troy that he is in danger.
Intending to renounce Troy, she in fact marries him,
fearing she may otherwise lose him. She allows Troy
to cloud her judgement and conscience.

Notice Bathsheba's
gradual loss of
vitality after her
marriage to Troy.

However, once married, she quickly becomes aware of
his 'faults' (p. 330), but she loses control of the farm.
She appreciates Gabriel's loyalty in saving the ricks. She
feels increasingly powerless, pleading in vain with Troy
to stop gambling and burn Fanny's hair. **Ironically** (see
Literary Terms), she experiences the torment of
jealousy, like Boldwood. Pity prevails when Bathsheba
views Fanny and the baby in the coffin, but Troy's
rejection and refusal to kiss her hurt.

She regains her dignity and pride, refusing to be a
'runaway wife' (p. 366) and respecting Fanny's memory.
Although Troy is presumed dead, she feels that he is
alive and will return. As a deserted wife she loses
interest in the farm, appointing Gabriel as bailiff. More
mature and reflective, she views her past conduct as
'inexcusable, wicked' (p. 412); she allows Boldwood to
propose again. **Ironically** on the night she gives her
promise, the shocked scream she emits, when Troy
attempts to reclaim her, provokes Boldwood to shoot
Troy.

After Troy's death she becomes weak and depressed
and increasingly dependent on Gabriel. Realising that
she loves him, she agrees to marry him.

GABRIEL OAK

Gabriel dominates the opening chapters. He is a 'young man of sound judgement' and 'general good character' (p. 51). He has worked hard to become an independent farmer. Although he is attracted to Bathsheba, he is quick to judge her as vain. This censorious streak is prevalent throughout the novel. He voices conventional Victorian morality.

Honest and hardworking

Practical and trustworthy

Faithful and strong

His picture of married bliss includes babies and togetherness 'at home by the fire' (p. 79). He accepts rejection gracefully, remaining constant in his love throughout the novel. Unselfishly he is relieved that Bathsheba does not have to share his poverty after his financial ruin.

He acts calmly and bravely in a crisis, saving Bathsheba's crops from fire in Chapter 6 and later from the storm. He accepts their reversed positions with dignity, when he becomes Bathsheba's shepherd, hiding his disappointment that he is not made bailiff.

Like an oak tree, Gabriel is solid and dependable.

The workmen, who admire his literacy and astronomical knowledge, respect him. He proves a worthy shepherd, caring for the weak lambs and acting successfully when the sheep become bloated from eating clover.

He honestly condemns Bathsheba's conduct to Boldwood on a number of occasions, twice facing dismissal. He is dismayed by Bathsheba's 'infatuation' with Troy, attempting to warn her against trusting him (he knows about the affair with Fanny). He hides his feelings – 'he adored Bathsheba' (p. 203). Hardy points up the contrast between 'homely Oak' and the attractive Troy whose 'deformities lay deep down from a woman's vision' (p. 244). Whereas Troy gambles, Gabriel reckons up the exact financial value of each rick threatened by the storm.

Consider why these characters trust Gabriel's judgement.

Both Bathsheba and Boldwood trust and confide in Gabriel: Bathsheba – the reasons for her secret marriage, and Boldwood – his disappointment and depression. Gabriel tries to prevent Bathsheba learning the truth by removing the chalked words about Fanny's child from the coffin. Later he advises Bathsheba to give Boldwood a conditional promise to marry him in six years' time. He loyally serves the widowed Bathsheba and manages the farm.

His industry is rewarded; he is appointed Bathsheba's bailiff, offered a share of the profits to manage Boldwood's farm and finally the tenancy of Boldwood's farm after his imprisonment. His constancy is also rewarded by Bathsheba's hand at the end of the story.

FANNY ROBIN

Fanny is a direct contrast to Bathsheba: she is blonde and fragile while Bathsheba is dark and lively. She is a shadowy figure adding mystery to the plot. Hardy **juxtaposes** (see Literary Terms) scenes with Troy and Fanny with Bathsheba. They only meet once on Yalbury Hill; Bathsheba discovers Fanny's identity when she opens the coffin.

Fanny first appears in Chapter 7, in Weatherbury churchyard (the place where she will finally be buried): 'a slim girl, rather thinly clad' (p. 99) with an unhealthy

Delicate and shy
Passive and weak
Unselfish and romantic

fast pulse. She is Bathsheba's youngest servant, who runs away to seek her soldier lover. She is depicted as a vulnerable 'little shape' (p. 135) in a hostile snowy landscape, as she appeals to Troy to honour his promise to marry her. When he prevaricates she becomes tearful rather than angry.

Ironically (see Literary Terms), her letter rejoicing in her forthcoming marriage is naïve and premature. Hardy evokes pity for Fanny when she muddles the churches and faces Troy's fury. She pleads in vain for another wedding day. She is a victim of circumstance, a shadowy presence who reveals Troy's fickleness when he flirts with Bathsheba.

Fanny conceals her pregnancy and supports herself as a seamstress until she goes to Casterbridge workhouse to have her baby. Hardy evokes pity by describing in harrowing detail her last journey, especially with the picture of her 'little arms' (p. 326) resting on the large dog. Her death, giving birth to her illegitimate baby, is deliberately understated in contrast to the **melodramatic** (see Literary Terms) death of Troy.

Ironically she has more power in death than in life. Her beauty in the coffin reduces Troy to abject shame and reawakens his love, so that he leaves Bathsheba.

SERGEANT FRANCIS TROY

Hardy contrasts Gabriel and Troy: Oak looked 'like a candle beside gas' (p. 299). Troy is attractive but unstable. We first see Troy with Fanny in Chapter 11. He treats her carelessly, leaving her out in the snow to find her own lodgings. Later his pride is wounded by her failure to arrive at the church for their wedding.

Boldwood describes Troy's antecedents: possibly the illegitimate son of an aristocrat, his French mother gave birth to him soon after marrying a doctor. Although well educated he had 'the wild freak of enlisting' (p. 161). Hardy's harsh **authorial comments** (see Literary Terms) in Chapter 25 present Troy as a hedonist, a fluent liar and flatterer of women.

Handsome and unstable

A romantic liar

Fickle

His whirlwind courtship of Bathsheba is romantic and dangerous (see Style). They meet in summer outdoors: at night outside her house, in the fields, hiving the bees and secretly in the evening for the sword exercise.

Attracted by her beauty he subdues her by flattery.
Neither Gabriel nor Boldwood praise her beauty.
His timely absence in Bath increases her fear of
losing him, which he exploits, threatening to leave her
for another woman unless she agrees to a secret
marriage.

He tricks Boldwood into believing he can be bribed
first to marry Fanny and then Bathsheba. When he
finally gives Boldwood the newspaper announcement of
his marriage, he makes Boldwood a dangerous enemy.
He purchases his discharge from the army and becomes
the improvident master of the farm. He treats

Troy treats
Bathsheba badly
after they are
married.

Bathsheba as carelessly as Fanny, ignoring her pleas to
stop gambling and not give the workmen strong drink.
The disastrous wedding feast is a **parody** (see Literary
Terms) of the shearing supper.

He excites Bathsheba's curiosity and jealousy by
refusing to name the woman on Yalbury Hill or
destroy Fanny's hair. He is 'gentle' to Fanny, castigating
himself as a 'brute' (p. 320), although angry when
Fanny fails to arrive at Grey's Bridge. He shows tender
'remorse' and 'reverence' (p. 360) to the dead Fanny and
child, but cruelly refuses to kiss Bathsheba.

His attempts at reparation are doomed to failure. A
storm stains the tombstone and washes away the
flowers. Hardy exposes the 'futility' of Troy's romantic
actions. The depressed Troy nearly drowns in Lulwind
Cove. His disappearance paves the way for Boldwood's
second proposal.

Notice how Troy is
a master of disguise.

Like the villain of a **melodrama** (see Literary Terms)
he reappears in various disguises. At Greenhill Fair he
enjoys risks, playing Turpin in front of Bathsheba.
Then disguised by a beard he steals Pennyways's note
and waylays Pennyways. Seeing Bathsheba with
Boldwood he is excited by her beauty and jealous. He is

also mercenary: tired of his life as a 'needy adventurer' (p. 427) he wishes to reclaim her.

His last appearance, disguised in a large overcoat, is at Boldwood's Christmas party. He roughly seizes Bathsheba's arm, provoking Boldwood to shoot him.

MR BOLDWOOD

Boldwood, the third suitor, is a contrast to both Gabriel and Troy. He is Bathsheba's neighbour, a rich gentleman farmer and bachelor of forty. He was kind to the friendless child Fanny, paying for her education and obtaining a post for her as servant.

His past is mysterious. Rumour says that he was 'jilted'. Indifferent to Bathsheba and all previous women, a natural 'celibate' (p. 170), after receiving Bathsheba's fatal Valentine he becomes obsessed with 'tropic

Reserved and
intense

Moody and
passionate

intensity' (p. 171). He quickly falls in love and proposes, offering Bathsheba a lady's life of leisure. He refuses to accept rejection, proposing again after the shearing supper in a 'passionate scene' (p. 210). He tactfully allows her time to deliberate, expecting a favourable answer by harvest time.

It is fate that Troy arrives in his absence, arousing Bathsheba's love. Boldwood refuses to accept Bathsheba's letter of rejection. He pleads with her in vain at Yalbury Hill, reproaching her for giving him hope by sending the Valentine. He imagines public mockery, envisaging the loss of his 'good name' and 'standing' (p. 261). He is wild with jealousy when he guesses the truth and curses Troy. He calls to apologise but Bathsheba refuses to see him.

He desperately tries to bribe Troy to marry Fanny, but overhearing Bathsheba address Troy lovingly at night and fearing she is compromised he offers the money to

marry Bathsheba instead. When Troy shows Boldwood
the newspaper cutting his mocking laughter makes
Boldwood vow revenge. He becomes unbalanced,
carelessly forgetting to cover his ricks, so they are
damaged by the storm. Gabriel is shocked by
Boldwood's skull-like appearance. Boldwood like
Bathsheba confides in Gabriel.

Notice how
Boldwood's love
turns to obsession
and madness.

After Troy's death his feelings veer to wild hope. He
proposes again, agreeing to wait six years for Bathsheba.
He presses his suit vehemently, ignoring the fact that
she does not love him and agreeing to wait again until
Christmas. In the interim he buys an entire trousseau
and an engagement ring. He is generous to Gabriel the
disappointed suitor, offering him a larger share of the
profits for managing his farm. He refuses to listen to
Gabriel's warnings. At the party his happiness when
Bathsheba agrees to marry him is short lived: Troy
returns and with 'gnashing despair' (p. 439) Boldwood
shoots him. He attempts suicide and voluntarily
surrenders himself at Casterbridge gaol. At the last
moment his death sentence is changed to life
imprisonment on the grounds of insanity.

In the plot by shooting Troy he leaves the way clear for
Gabriel and the happy ending.

MINOR CHARACTERS

The villagers are like a Greek chorus, explaining and
commenting on the action. Bathsheba's workmen meet
in Warren's Malthouse, which provides a warm cosy
place where the latest gossip and news are discussed.
They give their views of Bathsheba, their new mistress,
in Chapter 8, and later attempt to warn her that Troy is
alive at Boldwood's Christmas party. Bathsheba's
female servants voice their views on both Boldwood and
Troy.

They add realism and humour: Joseph needs little persuasion to get drunk at the Buck's Head, as Fanny dead in her coffin cannot possibly be offended.

The close relationships between many of the characters show the strong bonds of tradition in the rural community. Scenes such as the shearing in the barn and the shearing supper are both practical and aesthetically pleasing.

Warren	The maltster is a well-respected old man, the owner of the malthouse.
Jacob Poorgrass	The maltster's son, aged 65, his failing is 'multiplying eye' (p. 347) – double vision; a shy, saintly figure.
Liddy Smallbury	The maltster's granddaughter, Bathsheba's servant and companion. She advises Bathsheba to send the Valentine.
Cainy Ball	He becomes Gabriel's young undershepherd. He chokes comically trying to relate his news of Bathsheba and Troy in Bath.
Laban Tall	He is a shy hen-pecked man.
Jan Coggan	He offers Gabriel lodgings and rides with him in pursuit of the mysterious horse 'thief'.
Maryann, Temperance & Soberness	These are three female servants. They perform a wide variety of tasks throughout the rural year, including planting potatoes and feeding the threshing machine – a dangerous occupation for women.

LANGUAGE & STYLE

Hardy as **narrator** (see Literary Terms) presents his characters directly to the reader with detailed descriptions of their appearance, virtues and faults (Chapter 1 – Gabriel; Chapter 18 – Boldwood; Chapter 25 – Troy). He also uses characters to comment on each other, particularly Gabriel.

GABRIEL AS MORAL YARDSTICK

His limited viewpoint is **symbolised** (see Literary Terms) by his comic attempts to spy on Bathsheba in the opening chapters. He watches Bathsheba from behind a hedge, pronouncing her admiration of her reflection in a mirror as 'vanity'. From a hole in a shed he views her tending her aunt's cows. From his hut he espies her performing gymnastics on her horse.

Gabriel voices conventional Victorian morality. As the novel becomes more serious he observes Boldwood with Bathsheba at the sheep-washing pool and the shearing barn. He only hears fragments of their conversation before they move away, so his judgements are limited. Although Bathsheba confides in and respects Gabriel as an arbiter of 'morals' (p. 417), his views are always conventional. He roundly condemns her treatment of Boldwood as 'unworthy' (p. 185) and frankly tells her that Troy is 'not good enough' (p. 246) for her. Hardy's **authorial comments** (see Literary Terms) show the complexity of Bathsheba's emotions and often exonerate her from blame.

THE SIGNIFICANCE OF THE TITLE

Far from the Madding Crowd comes from Gray's 'Elegy written in a Country Churchyard'. The poem, while lamenting the obscure destiny of the hamlet's dead, consoles the dead, in that they have escaped the mad undignified rat race of the city.

The title is **ironic** (see Literary Terms). The novel shows the characters struggling and suffering, the maddened Boldwood commits murder; yet they live in idyllic rural surroundings.

HARDY'S USE OF LANGUAGE

The main characters are educated and speak standard
English. The workpeople (and Gabriel occasionally) use
Dorset **dialect** (see Literary Terms). Unlike William
Barnes, his contemporary Dorset poet, Hardy does not
write **dialect** phonetically. He regularises the spelling
while reproducing the different words and the rhythm
of the sentences. The workmen use archaic, old forms
such as 'a (he), ye (you), seed (saw) and completely
different words like 'gay jerry-go-nimble show' meaning
a colourful fair with booths and acrobats.

Hardy has a good ear for **dialogue** (see Literary
Terms). His novels are dramatic and translate well to
film and television.

SEXUAL SYMBOLISM

(See also Themes, A Feminist Perspective.)

Notice how all the Hardy uses weapons to **symbolise** (see Literary Terms)
suitors exhibit the power the suitors have to harm Bathsheba.
violent traits. • Gabriel subdues a frightened ewe; Bathsheba
comments that the newly sheared ewe's pink skin
resembles a woman who 'blushes at the insult'
(p. 197). The sheep emerging from its fleece is
compared to Aphrodite, the Greek goddess of beauty
and sexual love. Gabriel accidentally wounds another
'sheep in the groin', because he is distracted by
jealousy watching Bathsheba with Boldwood
• Boldwood's clumsy, aggressive pursuit of Bathsheba
is likened to 'a battering ram' (p. 394)
• Troy's spur gets caught in her dress; his sword splits a
caterpillar on her breast and cuts off a lock of her hair

Constrained by Victorian censorship, Hardy subtly
hints that Bathsheba is sexually attracted to Troy. She
earlier rejected Gabriel, stating she wanted 'somebody

to tame her' (p. 80). Troy's handsome appearance has
the effect of a 'fairy transformation' (p. 214). Troy
Notice the contrast physically traps Bathsheba with his spur. Although she
between struggles to escape, Hardy comments on her desire 'to
Bathsheba's be mastered' (p. 218). She enjoys the danger and close
passivity and physical proximity of their encounters. She is thrilled by
Troy's aggressive the sword exercise 'powerless to withstand or deny him'
masculinity. (p. 241). Finally, his red uniform disappears 'in a flash
like a brand', the **simile** (see Literary Terms) suggests
the harmful nature of the passion he has aroused.
Bathsheba feels flushed, tearful and sinful after he has
kissed her.

THE USE OF PATHETIC FALLACY

Hardy creates atmosphere by his descriptions of
landscape and weather. Nature can harmonise with
human concerns, but it can also prove a hostile
threatening force.

After Gabriel has lost his sheep the landscape of
Norcombe Hill reflects his despair. The moon is an
'attenuated skeleton'; the pond 'glittered like a dead
man's eye' (p. 87). Bathsheba spends the night outdoors
after Troy has left her. Her mood of despair and
destructive jealousy of Fanny is crystallised by the
'malignant' swamp, where fungi grow from 'rotting
leaves'. This hollow is a 'nursery of pestilence' (p. 363);
whereas the hollow in which Troy showed her the
magical sword exercise had ferns with 'soft feathery
arms caressing her' (p. 237).

VISUAL IMAGES

Most of the novel is set out of doors, only four places
are described in detail: Bathsheba's house, the shearing
barn, the cornmarket and Warren's Malthouse.

*Notice how Hardy uses what would nowadays be considered as filmic **devices** (see Literary Terms): alternating panoramic and close-up shots.*

Hardy often uses a panoramic view and then focuses on small specific details, like a film camera.

- The morning after Boldwood receives the Valentine, he watches the sun rising over the hill onto Bathsheba's farm and the snowy land 'like a red and flameless fire shining over a white hearthstone'. The moon fading in the west looks 'like tarnished brass'. In the distance on the ridge he sees a figure ... 'carrying skeleton masses' followed by another 'small figure on all fours' (pp. 151–2). This is Gabriel carrying sheep hurdles followed by his dog. The strange 'preternatural inversion of light and shade' suggests the abnormality of Boldwood's emotional state.

- The storm on the ill-fated harvest supper is a memorable episode due to Hardy's skilful descriptions. Hardy begins with a panoramic shot of the sky. The moon is 'lurid and metallic', the fields 'sallow with the impure light' of the approaching storm. Later he focuses on the drunken revel inside the barn, giving the scene the qualities of hell. The darkness is fitfully illuminated by the few remaining candles, others 'smoked and stank, grease dropping' on the floor. In the middle of the drunk unconscious workmen, Troy 'shone red and distinct' (p. 302). Outside again Hardy likens the lightning striking to the 'dance of death' with 'the forms of skeletons' and 'snakes of green'. Gabriel thatching at the top of a rick appears small and insignificant 'in such close juxtaposition with an infuriated universe' (pp. 308–9).

The writing is poetic in its intensity and clearly demonstrates why Hardy is such a famous writer.

PART FOUR

STUDY SKILLS

HOW TO USE QUOTATIONS

One of the secrets of success in writing essays is the way you use quotations. There are five basic principles:

- Put inverted commas at the beginning and end of the quotation
- Write the quotation exactly as it appears in the original
- Do not use a quotation that repeats what you have just written
- Use the quotation so that it fits into your sentence
- Keep the quotation as short as possible

Quotations should be used to develop the line of thought in your essays.

Your comment should not duplicate what is in your quotation. For example:

> Gabriel ignores Coggan's advice to flatter Troy, preferring to risk dismissal.
>
> 'I can't flatter, and if my place here is only to be kept by smoothing him down, my place must be lost' (p. 296).

Far more effective is to write:

> Gabriel rejects Coggan's advice: 'I can't flatter, and if my place here is only to be kept by smoothing him down, my place must be lost'.

However, the most sophisticated way of using the writer's words is to embed them into your sentence:

> Gabriel proudly rejects Coggan's advice to 'flatter' Troy, preferring the risk of losing his 'place'.

When you use quotations in this way, you are demonstrating the ability to use text as evidence to support your ideas - not simply including words from the original to prove you have read it.

Everyone writes differently. Work through the suggestions given here and adapt the advice to suit your own style and interests. This will improve your essay-writing skills and allow your personal voice to emerge.

The following points indicate in ascending order the skills of essay writing:

- Picking out one or two facts about the story and adding the odd detail
- Writing about the text by retelling the story
- Retelling the story and adding a quotation here and there
- Organising an answer which explains what is happening in the text and giving quotations to support what you write

....

- Writing in such a way as to show that you have thought about the intentions of the writer of the text and that you understand the techniques used
- Writing at some length, giving your viewpoint on the text and commenting by picking out details to support your views
- Looking at the text as a work of art, demonstrating clear critical judgement and explaining to the reader of your essay how the enjoyment of the text is assisted by literary devices, linguistic effects and psychological insights; showing how the text relates to the time when it was written

The dotted line above represents the division between lower- and higher-level grades. Higher-level performance begins when you start to consider your response as a reader of the text. The highest level is reached when you offer an enthusiastic personal response and show how this piece of literature is a product of its time.

Coursework
essay

Set aside an hour or so at the start of your work to plan what you have to do.

- List all the points you feel are needed to cover the task. Collect page references of information and quotations that will support what you have to say. A helpful tool is the highlighter pen: this saves painstaking copying and enables you to target precisely what you want to use.
- Focus on what you consider to be the main points of the essay. Try to sum up your argument in a single sentence, which could be the closing sentence of your essay. Depending on the essay title, it could be a statement about a character: Our first impression of Gabriel is 'he was a young man of sound judgement, easy motions, proper dress, and general good character'; an opinion about setting: Yalbury Hill at dusk provides a fitting mysterious setting for Troy's re-encounter with Fanny; or a judgement on a theme: Fate is a key theme in the novel. The fatal timing of Troy's reappearance coinciding with Boldwood's jealousy contributes to his tragic death.
- Make a short essay plan. Use the first paragraph to introduce the argument you wish to make. In the following paragraphs develop this argument with details, examples and other possible points of view. Sum up your argument in the last paragraph. Check you have answered the question.
- Write the essay, remembering all the time the central point you are making.
- On completion, go back over what you have written to eliminate careless errors and improve expression. Read it aloud to yourself, or, if you are feeling more confident, to a relative or friend.

If you can, try to type your essay, using a word processor. This will allow you to correct and improve your writing without spoiling its appearance.

Examination essay

The essay written in an examination often carries more marks than the coursework essay even though it is written under considerable time pressure.

In the revision period build up notes on various aspects of the text you are using. Fortunately, in acquiring this set of York Notes on *Far from the Madding Crowd*, you have made a prudent beginning! York Notes are set out to give you vital information and help you to construct your personal overview of the text.

Make notes with appropriate quotations about the key issues of the set text. Go into the examination knowing your text and having a clear set of opinions about it.

In most English Literature examinations you can take in copies of your set books. This is an enormous advantage although it may lull you into a false sense of security. Beware! There is simply not enough time in an examination to read the book from scratch.

In the examination

- Read the question paper carefully and remind yourself what you have to do.
- Look at the questions on your set texts to select the one that most interests you and mentally work out the points you wish to stress.
- Remind yourself of the time available and how you are going to use it.
- Briefly map out a short plan in note form that will keep your writing on track and illustrate the key argument you want to make.
- Then set about writing it.
- When you have finished, check through to eliminate errors.

To summarise, these are the keys to success:

- **Know the text**
- **Have a clear understanding of and opinions on the storyline, characters, setting, themes and writer's concerns**
- **Select the right material**
- **Plan and write a clear response, continually bearing the question in mind**

SAMPLE ESSAY PLAN

A typical essay question on *Far from the Madding Crowd* is followed by a sample essay plan in note form. This does not present the only answer to the question, merely one answer. Do not be afraid to include your own ideas and leave out some of the ones in this sample! Remember that quotations are essential to prove and illustrate the points you make.

Explore Hardy's use of letters in *Far from the Madding Crowd*. Do you think they are successful literary devices?

Introduction   Letters advance the plot and also reveal a great deal about the characters in their reactions to them whether they are sending or receiving them.

Part 1   Bathsheba sends Boldwood a Valentine. Note the contrast between the playful mood in which it was sent and Boldwood's dramatic reaction on receiving it.

Part 2   Give a short account of the way Boldwood's obsessive love develops: watches the sunrise the next day, looks intently at Bathsheba in the cornmarket and is jealous of another farmer; his first proposal; Gabriel's criticism of Bathsheba for sending the Valentine; Bathsheba's guilt. After the second proposal she gives Boldwood hope he'll be accepted by harvest time.

Part 3   Brief account of the contents of Fanny's letter: contrast her belief Troy will marry her with Boldwood's distrust; note Gabriel shows this letter to Boldwood disregarding Fanny's request for secrecy. Importance in the plot; later Boldwood tries to bribe Troy to marry Fanny.

Part 4   Bathsheba writes an emotional postscript in her letter, requesting Gabriel to return and lance her bloated sheep. She exploits her femininity and Gabriel's love. It's fate that she is forced to rescind his dismissal.

Part 5   Bathsheba tries to reject Boldwood by letter, a cowardly action. Later she has to face him on Yalbury Hill. Note her immense regret for sending the Valentine; **ironically** it's too late to apologise.

Part 6   Gabriel's letter of resignation and his decision to emigrate shock Bathsheba out of her depression; leads to Gabriel's second proposal and their marriage at the end.

Conclusion   Letters have a fatal and decisive effect on the characters' lives and destinies. Bathsheba's guilt about the Valentine leads her to postpone her answer to Boldwood's proposals; **ironically**, it would have been kinder to reject Boldwood straight away, like Gabriel. Boldwood's love leads him to kill Troy and attempt suicide. Decide whether the letters are an obtrusive plot **device** or reveal latent weaknesses in the characters.

FURTHER QUESTIONS

Make a plan as shown above and attempt these questions.

1 'Bathsheba is an attractive lively heroine.' Do you agree?

2 Consider the rival claims of Gabriel, Boldwood and Troy to be the hero of the story.

3 Compare and contrast Bathsheba and Fanny. Discuss the importance of Fanny in the novel.

4 'Weatherbury was immutable.' Show how Hardy establishes the theme of rural tradition in the novel.

5 What use does Hardy make of settings at Norcombe Hill and at Casterbridge?

6 Which do you consider to be the two most dramatic scenes?

7 Contrast Boldwood's courtship of Bathsheba with Troy's. Explain why Troy is so successful.

8 By close reference to two or three incidents, show
   how Hardy uses landscape and weather to create
   atmosphere.
9 'Troy behaves like a villain in a melodrama.' Is this
   an adequate description of his role in the novel?
10 Explore Hardy's use of symbolism in the novel.
11 Consider why the novel is easily translated into the
   medium of film. Refer to particular adaptations you
   have seen.
12 'The ending is rushed and unconvincing.' Does the
   novel rely too heavily on coincidences?
13 Examine the function of the villagers in *Far from the
   Madding Crowd*.
14 Discuss Hardy's presentation of the theme of love
   and marriage.
15 Some Victorian readers condemned Bathsheba as a
   'hussy', who did not deserve to win Gabriel as a
   husband. Do you agree?
16 Write your own alternative ending in the style of
   Hardy. Add a short commentary analysing your
   work.
17 Bathsheba describes herself and Fanny as Troy's
   'victims'. How far are their sufferings the result of
   their own actions or a malevolent fate?
18 Examine the treatment of romance in *Far from the
   Madding Crowd* and in a modern novel.
19 Compare the happy ending of *Far from the Madding
   Crowd* with the ending of a modern short story.
20 'Valentines are traditional symbols of love.'
   Consider the views of the characters and/or authors
   in *Far from the Madding Crowd* and in two modern
   poems.
21 Compare Hardy's description of the storm in
   Chapters 36–8 with the writing about a storm in a
   modern novel or poem.

PART FIVE

CULTURAL CONNECTIONS

BROADER PERSPECTIVES

The novel translates well into film: as we have seen Hardy used filmic devices (see Literary Terms) before film existed.

It is helpful to watch the 1967 film of the novel, directed by John Schlesinger. It is largely faithful to the text, incorporating much of Hardy's dialogue, although Gabriel's sheep jump to their deaths over a cliff into the sea! The film contains many dramatic scenes, particularly the Christmas party in which Peter Finch as Boldwood gives a sensitive and moving performance. The film makes more explicit the sexual attraction between Troy and Bathsheba. The camera also shows Bathsheba looking directly at Fanny's dead baby in the coffin. The Dorset locations are beautiful, although the sheep seem remarkably clean. Unfortunately Julie Christie as Bathsheba looks like a 1960s fashion model.

In 1998 ITV produced a four-part dramatisation of the novel. Paloma Baeza as Bathsheba looked appropriately dark and sultry, but lacked vivacity. The adaptation contained some beautiful, lyrical scenes of village life, although the landscape was obviously not Dorset – the hills were far too rugged, steep and bare. There was a full complement of rural characters, who contributed humour and earthly wisdom. Fanny Robin's final journey to the workhouse was extremely harrowing. However, some extra modern dialogue, which made explicit the sexual feelings of the suitors, was rather unconvincing. The film was redeemed by the touching union of Gabriel and Bathsheba at the end.

The following books provide useful historical and social background: J. Fowles and J. Draper's *Thomas Hardy's England* (Cape, 1984); T. Sullivan's *Thomas Hardy: An Illustrated Biography* (Papermac, 1981).

For local topography and atmosphere, read and walk the six-mile area around 'Weatherbury' in Ann-Marie Edwards's *Discovering Hardy's Wessex* (Arcady, 1982).

Interesting critical works include: R. Morgan's *Women and Sexuality in the novels of Thomas Hardy* (Routledge, 1988); I. Gregor's *The Great Web* (Faber & Faber, 1974); A. Enstice's *Thomas Hardy: Landscapes of the Mind* (Macmillan, 1979).

LITERARY TERMS

authorial comment the view of the writer
device a literary method or technique
dialect local speech
images word pictures
irony the writer says one thing while implying the opposite; **dramatic irony** the reader knows more information than the characters; **prophetic irony** by chance the characters predict the future
juxtaposition placing ideas or things side by side for emphasis
melodrama a story or play where the characters' emotions are exaggerated
metaphor an implied comparison
narrator the writer telling the story

parody an imitation intended to mock or ridicule
pathetic fallacy the surrounding landscape, weather and atmosphere reflect the particular mood of the character or event
simile a comparison of two things introduced by 'like' or 'as'
symbol something that comes to represent something else by association; often an object that represents something abstract, such as an idea, quality or condition
tragic a sad or serious event often resulting in disaster or death

TEST ANSWERS

TEST YOURSELF (Chapters 1–5)

A
1 Gabriel
••• 2 Bathsheba
3 Bathsheba's aunt
4 Bathsheba
5 Gabriel
6 Bathsheba

TEST YOURSELF (Chapters 6–19)

A
1 Fanny
••• 2 Bathsheba
3 Troy
4 Gabriel
5 Boldwood
6 Boldwood

TEST YOURSELF (Chapters 20–33)

A
1 Gabriel
••• 2 Troy
3 Bathsheba
4 Gabriel

5 Boldwood
6 Gabriel
7 Boldwood
8 Troy

TEST YOURSELF (Chapters 34–46)

A
1 Boldwood
••• 2 Gabriel
3 Bathsheba
4 Fanny
5 Troy
6 Bathsheba

TEST YOURSELF (Chapters 47–57)

A
1 Bathsheba
••• 2 Boldwood
3 Troy
4 Gabriel
5 Bathsheba
6 Fanny
7 Boldwood

OTHER TITLES

GCSE and equivalent levels

Maya Angelou
I Know Why the Caged Bird Sings

Jane Austen
Pride and Prejudice

Alan Ayckbourn
Absent Friends

Elizabeth Barrett Browning
Selected Poems

Robert Bolt
A Man for All Seasons

Harold Brighouse
Hobson's Choice

Charlotte Brontë
Jane Eyre

Emily Brontë
Wuthering Heights

Shelagh Delaney
A Taste of Honey

Charles Dickens
David Copperfield

Charles Dickens
Great Expectations

Charles Dickens
Hard Times

Charles Dickens
Oliver Twist

Roddy Doyle
Paddy Clarke Ha Ha Ha

George Eliot
Silas Marner

George Eliot
The Mill on the Floss

William Golding
Lord of the Flies

Oliver Goldsmith
She Stoops To Conquer

Willis Hall
The Long and the Short and the Tall

Thomas Hardy
Far from the Madding Crowd

Thomas Hardy
The Mayor of Casterbridge

Thomas Hardy
Tess of the d'Urbervilles

Thomas Hardy
The Withered Arm and other Wessex Tales

L.P. Hartley
The Go-Between

Seamus Heaney
Selected Poems

Susan Hill
I'm the King of the Castle

Barry Hines
A Kestrel for a Knave

Louise Lawrence
Children of the Dust

Harper Lee
To Kill a Mockingbird

Laurie Lee
Cider with Rosie

Arthur Miller
The Crucible

Arthur Miller
A View from the Bridge

Robert O'Brien
Z for Zachariah

Frank O'Connor
My Oedipus Complex and other stories

George Orwell
Animal Farm

J.B. Priestley
An Inspector Calls

Willy Russell
Educating Rita

Willy Russell
Our Day Out

J.D. Salinger
The Catcher in the Rye

William Shakespeare
Henry IV Part 1

William Shakespeare
Henry V

William Shakespeare
Julius Caesar

William Shakespeare
Macbeth

William Shakespeare
The Merchant of Venice

William Shakespeare
A Midsummer Night's Dream

William Shakespeare
Much Ado About Nothing

William Shakespeare
Romeo and Juliet

William Shakespeare
The Tempest

William Shakespeare
Twelfth Night

George Bernard Shaw
Pygmalion

Mary Shelley
Frankenstein

R.C. Sherriff
Journey's End

Rukshana Smith
Salt on the snow

John Steinbeck
Of Mice and Men

Robert Louis Stevenson
Dr Jekyll and Mr Hyde

Jonathan Swift
Gulliver's Travels

Robert Swindells
Daz 4 Zoe

Mildred D. Taylor
Roll of Thunder, Hear My Cry

Mark Twain
Huckleberry Finn

James Watson
Talking in Whispers

William Wordsworth
Selected Poems

A Choice of Poets

Mystery Stories of the Nineteenth Century including The Signalman

Nineteenth Century Short Stories

Poetry of the First World War

Six Women Poets

York Notes Advanced

Margaret Atwood
The Handmaid's Tale

Jane Austen
Mansfield Park

Jane Austen
Persuasion

Jane Austen
Pride and Prejudice

Alan Bennett
Talking Heads

William Blake
Songs of Innocence and of Experience

Charlotte Brontë
Jane Eyre

Emily Brontë
Wuthering Heights

Geoffrey Chaucer
The Franklin's Tale

Geoffrey Chaucer
General Prologue to the Canterbury Tales

Geoffrey Chaucer
The Wife of Bath's Prologue and Tale

Joseph Conrad
Heart of Darkness

Charles Dickens
Great Expectations

John Donne
Selected Poems

George Eliot
The Mill on the Floss

F. Scott Fitzgerald
The Great Gatsby

E.M. Forster
A Passage to India

Brian Friel
Translations

Thomas Hardy
The Mayor of Casterbridge

Thomas Hardy
Tess of the d'Urbervilles

Seamus Heaney
Selected Poems from Opened Ground

Nathaniel Hawthorne
The Scarlet Letter

James Joyce
Dubliners

John Keats
Selected Poems

Christopher Marlowe
Doctor Faustus

Arthur Miller
Death of a Salesman

Toni Morrison
Beloved

William Shakespeare
Antony and Cleopatra

William Shakespeare
As You Like It

William Shakespeare
Hamlet

William Shakespeare
King Lear

William Shakespeare
Measure for Measure

William Shakespeare
The Merchant of Venice

William Shakespeare
Much Ado About Nothing

William Shakespeare
Othello

William Shakespeare
Romeo and Juliet

William Shakespeare
The Tempest

William Shakespeare
The Winter's Tale

Mary Shelley
Frankenstein

Alice Walker
The Color Purple

Oscar Wilde
The Importance of Being Earnest

Tennessee Williams
A Streetcar Named Desire

John Webster
The Duchess of Malfi

W.B. Yeats
Selected Poems

Chinua Achebe
Things Fall Apart

Edward Albee
Who's Afraid of Virginia Woolf?

Margaret Atwood
Cat's Eye

Jane Austen
Emma

Jane Austen
Northanger Abbey

Jane Austen
Sense and Sensibility

Samuel Beckett
Waiting for Godot

Robert Browning
Selected Poems

Robert Burns
Selected Poems

Angela Carter
Nights at the Circus

Geoffrey Chaucer
The Merchant's Tale

Geoffrey Chaucer
The Miller's Tale

Geoffrey Chaucer
The Nun's Priest's Tale

Samuel Taylor Coleridge
Selected Poems

Daniel Defoe
Moll Flanders

Daniel Defoe
Robinson Crusoe

Charles Dickens
Bleak House

Charles Dickens
Hard Times

Emily Dickinson
Selected Poems

Carol Ann Duffy
Selected Poems

George Eliot
Middlemarch

T.S. Eliot
The Waste Land

T.S. Eliot
Selected Poems

Henry Fielding
Joseph Andrews

E.M. Forster
Howards End

John Fowles
The French Lieutenant's Woman

Robert Frost
Selected Poems

Elizabeth Gaskell
North and South

Stella Gibbons
Cold Comfort Farm

Graham Greene
Brighton Rock

Thomas Hardy
Jude the Obscure

Thomas Hardy
Selected Poems

Joseph Heller
Catch-22

Homer
The Iliad

Homer
The Odyssey

Gerard Manley Hopkins
Selected Poems

Aldous Huxley
Brave New World

Kazuo Ishiguro
The Remains of the Day

Ben Jonson
The Alchemist

Ben Jonson
Volpone

James Joyce
A Portrait of the Artist as a Young Man

Philip Larkin
Selected Poems

D.H. Lawrence
The Rainbow

D.H. Lawrence
Selected Stories

D.H. Lawrence
Sons and Lovers

D.H. Lawrence
Women in Love

John Milton
Paradise Lost Bks I & II

John Milton
Paradise Lost Bks IV & IX

Thomas More
Utopia

Sean O'Casey
Juno and the Paycock

George Orwell
Nineteen Eighty-four

John Osborne
Look Back in Anger

Wilfred Owen
Selected Poems

Sylvia Plath
Selected Poems

Alexander Pope
Rape of the Lock and other poems

Ruth Prawer Jhabvala
Heat and Dust

Jean Rhys
Wide Sargasso Sea

William Shakespeare
As You Like It

William Shakespeare
Coriolanus

William Shakespeare
Henry IV Pt 1

William Shakespeare
Henry V

William Shakespeare
Julius Caesar

William Shakespeare
Macbeth

William Shakespeare
Measure for Measure

William Shakespeare
A Midsummer Night's Dream

William Shakespeare
Richard II

William Shakespeare
Richard III

William Shakespeare
Sonnets

William Shakespeare
The Taming of the Shrew

William Shakespeare
Twelfth Night

William Shakespeare
The Winter's Tale

George Bernard Shaw
Arms and the Man

George Bernard Shaw
Saint Joan

Muriel Spark
The Prime of Miss Jean Brodie

John Steinbeck
The Grapes of Wrath

John Steinbeck
The Pearl

Tom Stoppard
Arcadia

Tom Stoppard
Rosencrantz and Guildenstern are Dead

Jonathan Swift
Gulliver's Travels and The Modest Proposal

Alfred, Lord Tennyson
Selected Poems

W.M. Thackeray
Vanity Fair

Virgil
The Aeneid

Edith Wharton
The Age of Innocence

Tennessee Williams
Cat on a Hot Tin Roof

Tennessee Williams
The Glass Menagerie

Virginia Woolf
Mrs Dalloway

Virginia Woolf
To the Lighthouse

William Wordsworth
Selected Poems

Metaphysical Poets